The Quotable Historian

The Quotable Historian

Words of Wisdom from Winston Churchill,
Barbara Tuchman, Edward Gibbon,
Julius Caesar, David McCullough, and More

ALAN AXELROD

McGraw-Hill

New York   San Francisco   Washington, D.C.   Auckland   Bogotá
Caracas   Lisbon   London   Madrid   Mexico City   Milan
Montreal   New Delhi   San Juan   Singapore
Sydney   Tokyo   Toronto

McGraw-Hill

A Division of The McGraw-Hill Companies

1 2 3 4 5 6 7 8 9 0 DOC/DOC 0 9 8 7 6 5 4 3 2 1 0 9

ISBN 0-07-135733-5

Printed and bound by R. R. Donnelley & Sons Company.

McGraw-Hill books are available at special quantity discounts to use as premiums and sales promotions, or for use in corporate training programs. For more information, please write to the Director of Special Sales, Professional Publishing, McGraw-Hill, 2 Penn Plaza, New York, NY 10121-2298. Or contact your local bookstore.

This publication is designed to provide accurate and authoritative information in regard to the subject matter covered. It is sold with the understanding that neither the author nor the publisher is engaged in rendering legal, accounting, or other professional service. If legal advice or other expert assistance is required, the services of a competent professional person should be sought.
—*From a Declaration of Principles jointly adopted by a Committee of the American Bar Association and a Committee of Publishers.*

 This book is printed on recycled, acid-free paper containing a minimum of 50% recycled, de-inked fiber.

Foreword

"The past is a foreign country. People do things differently there." Or words to that effect. According to legend, this sexy sound bite was first uttered by the famous 1830s transcendentalist, Ralph Waldo Emerson. In a fit of nostalgia, he was trying to convince his fellow countrymen that America had lost its moral compass during the presidency of Andrew Jackson. Things had been so much simpler, more honest, and truer in the days of Washington, Jefferson, and Madison, Emerson suggested. Sadly, he knew that one can never go back to the good old days, and it depressed him enough to drop out and form his own escapist commune in the woods of Massachusetts. Over the years, American historians fell in love with his "foreign country" quip, although none of them could confirm he ever uttered it. It helps hip, live-for-today students in a history class relate to the behavior of people who died centuries ago. Indeed, the past is an alien place, and a real or imagined quote from a famous American thinker, like Emerson, can only help in the study of it.

Of course, politicians-turned-amateur historians have exploited quotes like Emerson's more than history teachers. John and Robert Kennedy could spew their own versions of Emerson at the drop of a hat, and always to justify bold, new civil rights or foreign policies. Republican Ronald Reagan, in turn, quoted John and Robert Kennedy to appeal to so-called Reagan Democrats. Throughout the 1980s, Reagan's cute one-liners plucked out of alleged speeches by the Kennedys had historians and the press scurrying to check his sources. In most cases, the quotes had never been made, but they helped bolster the image of Reagan, the Great Communicator. All's fair, someone once said, in love and politics.

If it's been said, and it made a difference after it was said, Alan Axelrod has the rest of the story for you. *The Quotable Historian* is about great words from great writers and speakers who have influenced all of us over the years. In these days of "Headline News" and snappy sound bites, great words are not as essential to the his-

torical profession as they used to be. It's an unfortunate development, and the prolific Alan Axelrod demonstrates why. He reminds
us that words are power, and that all of us will be powerless if we
cannot explain, analyze, and learn from the past. Remember, "the
past is a foreign country. People do things differently there." I wonder who really said that?

Timothy Maga
Oglesby Professor of American Heritage,
Bradley University

Contents

⇜ *To the Reader* ⇝

"Those who cannot remember the past," the philosopher George Santayana declared, "are condemned to repeat it." But Henry Ford observed, "History is more or less bunk." Somewhere between these extremes lie the truth and importance of history, the writing of history, and the study of history. And between these extremes, too, is the vast, rich range of opinion, observation, criticism, and crystallized wisdom of historians on the panorama of human events and on how we interpret them. At the threshold of a new millennium, *The Quotable Historian* is intended to bring together and present a sampling from this broad and engaging spectrum of experience and reflection, some of it emotionally intense, some of it celebratory, some of it profoundly inspiring, some of it bitter, some of it heartbreaking, and some of it wry or outright hilarious.

The quotations in this book have been chosen from the world's significant histories as well as from the offhand comments of the significant historians. But just who are the "significant historians"? Included here are those writers who built their careers primarily on the composition of narrative histories. However, also included are many other writers, including philosophers, poets, novelists, economists, and scientists, who also wrote history or who figure importantly in how professional historians think about history. Finally, the reader will also find quotations from some of the makers of history who also wrote about the subject, figures such as Julius Caesar, Theodore Roosevelt, Winston Churchill, and John F. Kennedy, to name four of the most prominent.

Most scholars agree that recorded history stretches back perhaps 5500 years, but *The Quotable Historian* begins before this, starting with Hesiod (8th century B.C.), then continuing with Herodotus (born about 484 B.C.) and Thucydides (born about 460 B.C. or earlier), and moving through the great Romans (Tacitus, Caesar, Polybius, Livy), the early Christian historians, and a few medieval historians. Renaissance historians and chroniclers had many colorful observations to make on the ways of the world as it awakened from the long slumber of the Dark Ages, but the truly great age of history begins in the eighteenth century with the incomparable Edward Gibbon (*Decline and Fall of the Roman Empire*), whose magisterial eloquence is amply represented here. The most popular nineteenth-century historians—among them Thomas Carlyle, Thomas Babington Macaulay, Francis Parkman, Jules Michelet, and Frederick Jackson Turner—present great riches to the seeker of pungent quotation. This is the age, too, of the fiction writer who doubles as a historian, and *The Quotable Historian* includes Washington Irving, James Fenimore Cooper, William Makepeace Thackeray, and others.

With the twentieth century, history becomes more specialized, and the reader will find quotations from practitioners of such specialties as African-American history, women's history, Native American history, the history of science, and military history, in addition to a host of modern popular historians, such as Barbara Tuchman, Shelby Foote, John Eisenhower, Alan Bullock, Eric Foner, and many others.

The Quotable Historian is arranged according to some of the leading themes that have most interested historians. This is intended to make the book most useful for the history student and the history buff, as well as for anyone who desires quick access to a trove of literate, incisive wisdom for the purpose of enlivening a speech, a classroom lesson, an essay, or merely for the pleasure of perusal.

Alan Axelrod

The Quotable Historian

 *Action*

The world can only be grasped by action, not by contemplation.
— JACOB BRONOWSKI (1908–1974), *The Ascent of Man,* 1973

The hand is the cutting edge of the mind.
— JACOB BRONOWSKI (1908–1974), *The Ascent of Man,* 1973

I came, I saw, I conquered.
— JULIUS CAESAR (100–44 B.C.), quoted in Suetonious, *Lives of the Caesars*

Talk that does not end in any kind of action is better suppressed altogether.
— THOMAS CARLYLE (1795–1881), speech, April 2, 1866

An ounce of action is worth a ton of theory.
— FRIEDRICH ENGELS (1820–1895), quoted in Reg Groves, *The Strange Case of Victor Grayson,* 1975

The first glance at History convinces us that the actions of men proceed from their needs, their passions, their characters and talents; and impresses us with the belief that such needs, passions and interests are the sole spring of actions.
— GEORG HEGEL (1770–1831), *The Philosophy of History,* 1837

These [Persian messengers] will not be hindered from accomplishing at their best speed the distance which they have to go, either by snow, or rain, or heat, or by the darkness of night.
— HERODOTUS (ca. 484–after 424 B.C.), *The Persian Wars;* adapted and adopted as the unofficial motto of the United States Postal Service

Force has no place where there is need of skill.
— HERODOTUS (ca. 484–after 424 B.C.), *Histories*

All truly great achievements in history resulted from the actualization of principles, not from the clever evaluation of political conditions.

— HENRY A. KISSINGER (1923–   ), *The Meaning of History: Reflections on Spengler, Toynbee and Kant*, 1950

Better late than never.

— LIVY (59 B.C.–A.D. 17), *History*

Somebody asked Theodore Roosevelt, "How have you been able to do all these things, write books, and run for public office, be a soldier, and be a naturalist, and be an outdoorsman, and so forth and so on?" And he said, "I put myself in the way of things happening, and things happen."

— DAVID MCCULLOUGH (1933–   ), quoting Theodore Roosevelt, interview with Roger Mudd, in *Great Minds of History*, 1999

One of my favorite quotes . . . was a remark attributed to an engineer named John Fritz, who was involved with the creation of the Bessemer steel process. One of the most important events in our history is the advent of cheap steel. It changed everything much more than any politician or any war. It changed the world. Well, Fritz was in Johnstown, Pennsylvania, and they built a machine for the new Bessemer process there. They had been working on it for months. Finally, he said, "All right, boys, she's done. Let's start her up, and see why she doesn't work."

— DAVID MCCULLOUGH (1933–   ), interview with Roger Mudd, in *Great Minds of History*, 1999

Drastic action may be costly, but it can be less expensive than continuing inaction.

— RICHARD E. NEUSTADT (1919–   ), *Presidential Power: The Politics of Leadership*, 1960

America and the American Character

American society is a sort of flat, fresh-water pond which absorbs silently, without reaction, anything which is thrown into it.
— HENRY BROOK ADAMS (1838–1918), letter, September 20, 1911

As for America, it is the ideal fruit of all your youthful hopes and reforms. Everybody is fairly decent, respectable, domestic, bourgeois, middle-class, and tiresome. There is absolutely nothing to revile except that it's a bore.
— HENRY BROOK ADAMS (1838–1918), letter, December 17, 1908

It is a noble land that God has given us: a land that can feed and clothe the world; a land whose coastlines would enclose half the countries of Europe; a land set like a sentinel between the two imperial oceans of the globe.
— ALBERT J. BEVERIDGE (1862–1927), speech, September 16, 1898

America has been a land of dreams. A land where the aspirations of people from countries cluttered with rich, cumbersome, aristocratic, ideological pasts can reach for what once seemed unattainable. Here they have tried to make dreams come true.... Yet now ... we are threatened by a new and particularly American menace. It is not the menace of class war, of ideology, of poverty, of disease, of illiteracy, or demagoguery, or of tyranny, though these now plague most of the world. It is the menace of unreality.
— DANIEL J. BOORSTIN (1914–   ), *The Image: A Guide to Pseudo-Events in America,* 1961

Until now, when we have started to talk about the uniqueness of America, we have almost always ended by comparing ourselves to Europe. Toward her we have felt all the attraction and repulsions of Oedipus.

    — DANIEL J. BOORSTIN (1914–   ), *America and the Image of Europe,* Foreword, 1960

Of all the nations in the world, the United States was built in nobody's image. It was the land of the unexpected, of unbounded hope, of ideals, of quest for an unknown perfection. It is all the more unfitting that we should offer ourselves in images. And all the more fitting that the images which we make wittingly or unwittingly to sell America to the world should come back to haunt and curse us.

    — DANIEL J. BOORSTIN (1914–   ), *The Image: A Guide to Pseudo-Events in America,* 1961

The most important lesson of American history is the promise of the unexpected. None of our ancestors would have imagined settling way over here on this unknown continent. So we must continue to have a society that is hospitable to the unexpected, which allows the possibilities to develop beyond our own imaginings.

    — DANIEL J. BOORSTIN (1914–   ), quoted in Tad Szulc, "The Greatest Danger We Face," *Parade Magazine,* 1993

The most important American addition to the world experience was the simple surprising fact of America. We have helped prepare mankind for all its later surprises.

    — DANIEL J. BOORSTIN (1914–   ), from a 1975 lecture quoted in *The Exploring Spirit: America and the World Experience,* 1976

The Indians knew that life was equated with the earth and its resources, that America was a paradise, and they could not comprehend why the intruders from the East were determined to destroy all that was Indian as well as America itself.

    — DEE BROWN (1908–   ), *Bury My Heart at Wounded Knee,* 1970

On the 15th of December they weighed anchor to go to the place they had discovered, and came within two leagues of it, but were fain to bear up again; but the 16th day, the wind came fair, and they arrived safe in this harbor. And afterwards took better view of the place, and resolved where to pitch their dwelling; and the 25th day began to erect the first house for common use to receive them and their goods.

— WILLIAM BRADFORD (1590–1657), *Of Plimoth Plantation*, 1647, describing the Pilgrims' landing at Plymouth

They knew they were pilgrims.

— WILLIAM BRADFORD (1590–1657), *Of Plimoth Plantation*, 1647

What then is the American, this new man? . . . *He* is an American, who, leaving behind him all his ancient prejudices and manners, receives new ones from the new mode of life he has embraced.

— J. HECTOR ST. JOHN DE CRÈVECOEUR (1735–1813), *Letters from an American Farmer*, 1782

. . . one cannot understand the intellectual equipment of the rising American nation without taking into account how the American physical environment and the new social environment modified the Old World intellectual agencies. . . . New Problems beget new thoughts.

— MERLE CURTI (1897–1996), *The Growth of American Thought*, 1943

The West begins where the average annual rainfall drops below 20 inches.

— BERNARD DE VOTO (1897–1955), *The Plundered Province*, 1934

The achieved West had given the United States something that no people had ever had before, an internal, domestic empire.

— BERNARD DE VOTO (1897–1955), *The Year of Decision*, 1943

America is the most grandiose experiment the world has seen, but, I am afraid, it is not going to be a success.

> — SIGMUND FREUD (1856–1939), quoted in Ronald W. Clark, *Freud: the Man and His Cause*, 1980

Yes, America is gigantic, but a gigantic mistake.

> — SIGMUND FREUD (1856–1939), remark to Ernest Jones, quoted in *Memories of a Psycho-analyst*, 1959

Ours is the only country deliberately founded on a good idea.

> — JOHN GUNTHER (1901–1970), *Inside USA*, 1947

America is, therefore, the land of the future, where, in the ages that lie before us, the burden of the world's history shall reveal itself. It is a land of desire for all those who are weary of the historical lumber-room of old Europe.

> — GEORG HEGEL (1770–1831), *The Philosophy of History*, 1832

There is one expanding horror in American life. It is that our long odyssey toward liberty, democracy and freedom-for-all may be achieved in such a way that utopia remains forever closed, and we live in freedom and hell, debased of style, not individual from one another, void of courage, our fear rationalized away.

> — NORMAN MAILER (1923–   ), *Cannibals and Christians*, 1966

I write the wonders of the Christian religion, flying from the depravations of Europe, to the American strand . . .

> — COTTON MATHER (1663–1728), *Magnalia Christi Americana*, 1702

The pastoral ideal has been used to define the meaning of America ever since the age of discovery, and it has not yet lost its hold upon the native imagination.

> — LEO MARX (1919–   ), *The Machine in the Garden: Technology and the Pastoral Ideal in America*, 1964

The strongest argument for the unmaterialistic character of American life is the fact that we tolerate conditions that are, from a negative point of view, intolerable. What the foreigner finds most objectionable in American life is its lack of basic comfort. No nation with any sense of material well-being would endure the food we eat, the cramped apartments we live in, the noise, the traffic, the crowded subways and buses. American life, in large cities, is a perpetual assault on the senses and the nerves; it is out of asceticism, out of unworldliness, precisely, that we bear it.

— MARY McCARTHY (1912–1989), 1947 essay reprinted in *On the Contrary,* 1961

America was discovered accidentally by a great seaman who was looking for something else; when discovered, it was not wanted; and most of the exploration for the next 50 years was done in the hope of getting around it.

— SAMUEL ELIOT MORISON (1887–1976), *The Oxford History of the American People,* 1965

The settlement of America had its origins in the unsettlement of Europe. America came into existence when the European was already so distant from the ancient ideas and ways of his birthplace that the whole span of the Atlantic did not widen the gulf.

— LEWIS MUMFORD (1895–1990), *The Golden Day,* 1926

The growth of New England was a result of the aggregate efforts of a busy multitude, each in his narrow circle toiling for himself, to gather competence or wealth. The expansion of New France was the achievement of a gigantic ambition striving to grasp a continent. It was a vain attempt.

— FRANCIS PARKMAN (1823–1893), *Pioneers of France in the New World,* 1865

The Puritan was a contribution of the old world, created by the rugged idealism of the English Reformation; the Yankee was a product of native conditions, created by a practical economy.

— VERNON L. PARRINGTON (1871–1929), *Main Currents in American Thought,* 1927

The things that will destroy America are prosperity-at-any-price, peace-at-any-price, safety-first instead of duty-first, the love of soft living, and the get-rich-quick theory of life.
— THEODORE ROOSEVELT (1858–1919), letter, January 10, 1917

American time has stretched around the world. It has become the dominant tempo of modern history, especially of the history of Europe.
— HAROLD ROSENBERG (1906–1978), *The Tradition of the New,* 1960

America is a young country with an old mentality.
— GEORGE SANTAYANA (1863–1952), *Winds of Doctrine,* 1913

It is veneer, rouge, aestheticism, art museums, new theaters, etc., that make America impotent. The good things are football, kindness, and jazz bands.
— GEORGE SANTAYANA (1863–1952), letter, May 22, 1927

America is a land of wonders, in which every thing is in constant motion and every change seems an improvement.
— ALEXIS DE TOCQUEVILLE (1805–1859), *Democracy in America,* 1840

I know of no country in which there is so little independence of mind and real freedom of discussion as in America.
— ALEXIS DE TOCQUEVILLE (1805–1859), *Democracy in America,* 1840

Two things in America are astonishing: the changeableness of most human behavior and the strange stability of certain principles. Men are constantly on the move, but the spirit of humanity seems almost unmoved.
— ALEXIS DE TOCQUEVILLE (1805–1859), *Democracy in America,* 1840

The whole life of an American is passed like a game of chance, a revolutionary crisis, or a battle.

➤ ALEXIS DE TOCQUEVILLE (1805–1859), *Democracy in America,* 1840

America is a large, friendly dog in a very small room. Every time it wags its tail, it knocks over a chair.

➤ A. J. TOYNBEE (1889–1975), radio broadcast news summaries, July 15, 1954

The gap between ideals and actualities, between dreams and achievements, the gap that can spur strong men to increased exertions, but can break the spirit of others—this gap is the most conspicuous, continuous landmark in American history. It is conspicuous and continuous not because Americans achieve little, but because they dream grandly. The gap is a standing reproach to Americans; but it marks them off as a special and singularly admirable community among the world's peoples.

➤ GEORGE F. WILL (1941–   ), *Statecraft as Soulcraft: What Government Does,* 1984

America lives in the heart of every man everywhere who wishes to find a region where he will be free to work out his destiny as he chooses.

➤ WOODROW WILSON (1856–1924), speech, April 6, 1912

Sometimes people call me an idealist. Well, that is the way I know I am an American. . . . America is the only idealistic nation in the world.

➤ WOODROW WILSON (1856–1924), speech, September 8, 1919

⟫ *American Revolution* ⟪

The heaviest calamity in English history, the breach with America, might never have occurred if George the Third had not been an honest dullard.

— SIR JAMES GEORGE FRAZER (1854–1941), *The Golden Bough*, 1922

It can never be forgotten that when the United States of America were colonies of Great Britain, they were part of an empire and responsive to happenings in other parts of the empire. When Great Britain went to war with France, British colonies automatically faced against neighboring French colonies and prepared defenses against the depredations of the French navy.

— FRANCIS JENNINGS (1918–   ), *Empire of Fortune: Crowns, Colonies, and Tribes in the Seven Years War in America*, 1988

For the first time since civilization dawned in the light of written language, a nation was born, based on freedom and justice for all and the belief that all men are created equal. . . . Its founders, with their love of Latin, called it *Novus Ordo Seculorum*—A New Order of the Ages—an ideal of perfection in representative government that, though not always attainable among imperfect human beings, nevertheless challenged, as it still does today, all the cruelties and injustices of fixed societies and despotisms everywhere.

— ROBERT LECKIE (1915–   ), *George Washington's War: The Saga of the American Revolution*, 1992

[In 1775,] the Americans revolted out of anticipated tyranny, rather than actual tyranny. They were frightened about the use of power.

— GORDON WOOD (1933–   ), interview with Roger Mudd, in *Great Minds of History*, 1999

The military struggle may frankly be regarded for what it actually was, namely a war for independence, an armed attempt to impose the views of the revolutionists upon the British government and large sections of the colonial population at whatever cost to freedom of opinion or the sanctity of life and property.

— ARTHUR SCHLESINGER (1888–1965), "The American Revolution Reconsidered," 1919, reprinted in *The Ambiguity of the American Revolution*, 1968

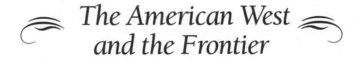

The American West and the Frontier

Someone has said that the West has been the mother of many children. Prominent among her offspring were the trapper, fur trader, prospector, freighter, cowboy, and homesteader. One by one these sons of a great mother were born, each lived out his allotted life span and passed away, and with the passing of the last one the mother herself must die.

— EDWARD EVERETT DALE (1879–1972), *Cow Country*, 1942

The myths of the West have been parented and nurtured by ideas of freedom, real and imagined, urgent and neurotic. When we start any new project in life—a new ranch, a marriage, a novel— we come to it with the best intentions and inspirations, but along with fierce energy and spontaneity come so much cultural baggage, habitual patterns, and preconceptions, we realize that freedom is, itself, a myth.

— GRETEL EHRLICH, "The West of True Myth," in Kathleen Jo Ryan, *Ranching Traditions: Legacy of the American West*, 1989

In real [western] gunfights . . . the primary consideration was not speed but accuracy. Gunfighters frequently did not even carry their weapons in holsters. Pistols were shoved into hip pockets, waistbands, or coat pockets, and a rifle or shotgun was almost always preferred over a handgun. The primary concern in a shootout was not hitting the other man first or in the right spot but just *hitting* him. . . . If western gunfighters were reincarnated today, they would be astonished by the emphasis on the fast draw; in their day it was so unimportant that it was hardly worth mentioning.

— BILL O'NEAL (1942–   ), *Encyclopedia of Western Gunfighters,* 1979

The frontier is . . . the meeting point between savagery and civilization . . . the line of most rapid and effective Americanization. The wilderness masters the colonist.

— FREDERICK JACKSON TURNER (1861–1932), *The Significance of the Frontier in American History,* 1894

. . . it's not so much that the West has more myths than the rest of the United States, but that the western myths stand for America in a way that myths about other sections don't. The South stands for the South. The East stands for the East as the oldest part, the founding of the United States. But the West stands for the American future. It's the place where America develops, where Americans become Americans. It's the place for whatever the United States is going to be. That's what the western myths have been about. Western myths are for everybody.

— RICHARD WHITE (1947–   ), interview with Roger Mudd, in *Great Minds of History,* 1999

The interesting thing is that the historical cowboy often worked for a corporation. He was hardly a lone individual—he worked for a wage. One of the interesting things is that he's the only wage earner I know who's become an iconic figure in the West. And most of the time, he chased cows. I mean, it was not particularly romantic labor.

— RICHARD WHITE (1947–   ), interview with Roger Mudd, in *Great Minds of History,* 1999

[Frederick Jackson Turner's frontier thesis] is very simple. Turner said that what made Americans was the existence of free land in the West, and it was the constant settlement of that free land, the retreat back to nature—back to barbarism almost—and then the recapitulation of progress out of this initial retreat that made Americans who they are. It made them democratic, it made them egalitarian, it made them optimistic. It made them a people who were ready and willing to take advantage of anything that life can put in their way. It also merged a fairly diverse group of immigrants into a single homogeneous group of people.

➤ RICHARD WHITE (1947–   ), interview with Roger Mudd, in *Great Minds of History*, 1999

 *Assassination*

You never know what's hit you. A gunshot is the perfect way.

➤ JOHN F. KENNEDY (1917–1963), quoted in Peter Collier and David Horowitz, *The Kennedys*, 1984

[On the assassination of Emperor Galba:] A shocking crime was committed on the unscrupulous initiative of few individuals, with the blessing of more, and amid the passive acquiescence of all.

➤ TACITUS (ca. 55–ca. 120), *The Histories*

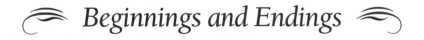 *Beginnings and Endings*

According to our chronology, [the creation of the world] fell upon the entrance of the night preceding the 23d day of October in the year of the Julian Calendar, 710 [that is, 4004 B.C.].

➤ JAMES USSHER (1581–1656), *The Annals of the World*, 1658

Who knows but that hereafter some traveler like myself will sit down upon the banks of the Seine, the Thames, or the Zuyder Zee, where now, in the tumult of enjoyment, the heart and the eyes are too slow to take in the multitude of sensations? Who knows but he will sit down solitary amid silent ruins, and weep a people inurned and their greatness changed into an empty name?

— CONSTANTIN DE VOLNEY (1757–1820), *Ruins*, 1791

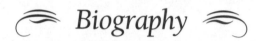

Biography

A well-written life is almost as rare as a well-spent one.

— THOMAS CARLYLE (1795–1881), "Jean Paul Friedrich Richter," 1827, reprinted in *Critical and Miscellaneous Essays*, 1839

If those gentlemen [the biographers] would let me alone, I should be much obliged to them. I would say, as Shakespeare would say . . . "Sweet friend, for Jesus' sake forbear."

— THOMAS CARLYLE (1795–1881), spoken in a conversation of 1868 and published in *A Diary*, 1907

No sooner does a great man depart, and leave his character as public property, than a crowd of little men rushes towards it. There they are gathered together, blinking up to it with such vision as they have, scanning it from afar, hovering round it this way and that, each cunningly endeavouring, by all arts, to catch some reflex of it in the little mirror of himself.

— THOMAS CARLYLE (1795–1881), "Jean Paul Friedrich Richter," 1827, reprinted in *Critical and Miscellaneous Essays*, 1839

The cruellest thing that has happened to Lincoln since he was shot by Booth has been to fall into the hands of Carl Sandburg.

— EDMUND WILSON (1895–1972), *Patriotic Gore*, 1962

 *Books*

The true university of these days is a collection of books.

— THOMAS CARLYLE (1795–1881), *On Heroes, Hero-Worship and the Heroic in History,* 1841

There are certain books in the world which every searcher for truth must know: the Bible, the *Critique of Pure Reason,* the *Origin of Species,* and Karl Marx's *Capital.*

— W. E. B. DU BOIS (1868–1963), *The Seventh Son,* 1933

Early in the morning, at break of day, in all the freshness and dawn of one's strength, to read a *book*—I call that vicious!

— FRIEDRICH NIETZSCHE (1844–1900), *Ecce Homo,* 1908

The worst readers are those who behave like plundering troops: they take away a few things they can use, dirty and confound the remainder, and revile the whole.

— FRIEDRICH NIETZSCHE (1844–1900), *Assorted Opinions and Maxims,* 1879

Education . . . has produced a vast population able to read but unable to distinguish what is worth reading, an easy prey to sensations and cheap appeals.

— G. M. TREVELYAN (1876–1962), *English Social History,* 1942

Books are the carriers of civilization. Without books, history is silent, literature dumb, science crippled, thought and speculation at a standstill.

— BARBARA TUCHMAN (1912–1989), *Author's League Bulletin,* November 1, 1979

To a historian, libraries are food, shelter, and even muse.

— BARBARA TUCHMAN (1912–1989), *Practicing History,* 1981

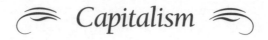

Capitalism

What breaks capitalism, all that will ever break capitalism, is capitalists: The faster they run, the more strain on their heart.
— RAYMOND WILLIAMS (1921–1988), *Loyalties,* 1985

Thomas Carlyle

[Thomas Carlyle] taught like one that had authority—a tone which men naturally resent, and must resent, till the teacher has made his pretensions good.
— JAMES A. FROUDE (1818–1894), *Thomas Carlyle: A History of His First Forty Years,* 1882

Thomas Carlyle is incontestably dead at last, by the acknowledgment of all newspapers. I had, however, the pleasure of an intimate intercourse with him when he was an infinitely deader man than he is now.
— HENRY JAMES, SR. (1811–1882), *Atlantic Monthly,* May 1881

Carlyle, a man of strong words and attitudes, a rhetorician from necessity, continually agitated by the desire for a strong faith and the feeling of incapacity for it (in this a typical Romantic!). . . . Carlyle is an English atheist who wants to be honored for not being one.
— FRIEDRICH NIETZSCHE (1844–1900), *Twilight of the Idols,* 1889

Rugged, mountainous, volcanic, he was himself more a French revolution than any of his volumes.
— WALT WHITMAN (1819–1892), *Specimen Days,* 1881

I could not help but say that Mr. Carlyle seemed the only virtuous philosopher we had. Upon which his wife answered, "My dear, if Mr. Carlyle's digestion had been stronger, there is no saying what he might have been!"

— MARGARET OLIPHANT (1828–1897), letter recounting a conversation with June Welsh Carlyle, 1866, reprinted in *Autobiography and Letters of Mrs. Margaret Oliphant*, 1899

The next work of Carlyle will be entitled "Bow-Wow," and the title page will have a motto from the opening chapter of the Koran: "There is *no* error in this Book."

— EDGAR ALLAN POE (1809–1845), *Marginalia*, 1849

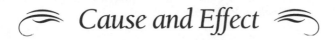 *Cause and Effect*

The present contains nothing more than the past, and what is found in the effect was already in the cause.

— HENRI BERGSON (1859–1941), *Creative Evolution*, 1907

Accident is something relative. It appears only at the point of intersection of *inevitable* processes.

— GEORGE PLEKHANOV (1856–1918), *The Role of the Individual in History*, 1898

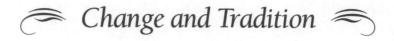 Change and Tradition

Only the fairy tale equates changelessness with happiness. Permanence means paralysis and death. Only in movement, with all its pain, is life.

— JACOB BURCKHARDT (1818–1897), "On Fortune and Misfortune in History," 1871, in *Judgements on History and Historians*, 1958

Nothing endures but change.

— HERACLITUS (ca. 540–ca. 480 B.C.), quoted in Diogenes Laertius, *Lives of Eminent Philosophers*

All is flux, nothing stays still.

— HERACLITUS (ca. 540–ca. 480 B.C.), quoted in Diogenes Laertius, *Lives of Eminent Philosophers*

There is nothing in the world more stubborn than a corpse: you can hit it, you can knock it to pieces, but you cannot convince it.

— ALEXANDER HERZEN (1812–1870), *My Past and Thoughts*, 1921

Constant revolutionizing of production . . . distinguishes the bourgeois epoch from all earlier ones. All fixed, fast-frozen relations, with their train of ancient and venerable prejudices, are swept away, all new-formed ones become antiquated before they can ossify. All that is solid melts into air, all that is holy is profaned, and man is at last compelled to face with sober senses, his real conditions of life, and his relations with his kind.

— KARL MARX (1818–1883) and FRIEDRICH ENGELS (1820–1895), *The Communist Manifesto*, 1848

Future shock [is] the shattering stress and disorientation that we induce in individuals by subjecting them to too much change in too short a time.

— ALVIN TOFFLER (1928–   ), *Future Shock*, 1970

There is a widespread assumption in modern social science that social conformity requires no explanation. Supposedly it is not problematical. Change is what requires explanation. . . . The assumption of inertia, that cultural and social continuity do not require explanation, obliterates the fact that both have to be recreated anew in each generation, often with great pain and suffering. To maintain and transmit a value system, human beings are punched, bullied, sent to jail, thrown into concentration camps, cajoled, bribed, made into heroes, encouraged to read newspapers, stood up against a wall and shot, and sometimes even taught sociology. To speak of cultural inertia is to overlook the concrete interests and privileges that are served by indoctrination, education, and the entire complicated process of transmitting culture from one generation to the next.

— Barrington Moore (1913–   ), *Social Origins of Dictatorship and Democracy,* 1966

A new consciousness, to free itself of the ubiquitous, pervasive presence of the old, must fiercely reject it, overreact, overstate (and pay a heavy price for doing so, like soldiers in a war in which no quarter is asked or given); but eventually they must always come back to make peace with all in the old order that gave them life and gave them the ideals in the name of which they wage war against it.

— Page Smith (1917–1995), *A New Age Now Begins,* 1976

I cannot help fearing that men may reach a point where they look on every new theory as a danger, every innovation as a toilsome trouble, every social advance as a first step toward revolution, and that they may absolutely refuse to move at all for fear of being carried off their feet. The prospect really does frighten me that they may finally become so engrossed in a cowardly love of immediate pleasures that their interest in their own future and in that of their descendants may vanish, and that they will prefer tamely to follow the course of their destiny rather than make a sudden energetic effort necessary to set things right.

— Alexis de Tocqueville (1805–1859), *Democracy in America,* 1840

Queen Victoria was like a great paper-weight that for half a century sat upon men's minds, and when she was removed, their ideas began to blow all over the place haphazardly.

— H. G. WELLS (1866–1946), quoted in Norman and Jean MacKenzie, *H. G. Wells*, 1973

Chaos Versus Order

Chaos often breeds life, when order breeds habit.

— HENRY BROOK ADAMS (1838–1918), *The Education of Henry Adams*, 1907

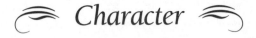

Character

It is not book learning young men need, not instruction about this and that, but a stiffening of the vertebrae which will cause them to be loyal to a trust, to act promptly, concentrate their energies, do a thing—"carry a message to Garcia."

— ELBERT HUBBARD (1856–1915), *A Message to Garcia*, 1899

It says nothing against the ripeness of a spirit that it has a few worms.

— FRIEDRICH NIETZSCHE (1844–1900), *Assorted Opinions and Maxims*, 1879

The soul is the captain and ruler of the life of mortals.

— SALLUST (86–34 B.C.), *The War with Jugurtha*

Noble character is best appreciated in those ages in which it can most readily develop.

— TACITUS (ca. 55–ca. 120), *Agricola*

We secure our friends not by accepting favors but by doing them.

— THUCYDIDES (ca. 460–400 B.C.), *The History of the Peloponnesian War*, 413 B.C.

If you will think about what you ought to do for other people, your character will take care of itself. Character is a by-product, and any man who devotes himself to its cultivation in his own case will become a selfish prig.

— WOODROW WILSON (1856–1924), speech, October 24, 1914

 *The Civil War*

The American people in 1860 believed they were the happiest and luckiest people in all the world, and in a way they were right.

— BRUCE CATTON (1899–1978), *The Civil War*, 1960

Here was the greatest and most moving chapter in American history, a blending of meanness and greatness, an ending and a beginning. It came out of what men were, but it did not go as men had planned it. The Almighty had His own purposes.

— BRUCE CATTON (1899–1978), *The Civil War*, 1960

"Tell them," [Jefferson Davis] paused as if to sort the words. "Tell the world that I only loved America," he said.

— JEFFERSON DAVIS (1808–1889), to a reporter, quoted in Shelby Foote, *Civil War: A Narrative*, 1974

The Civil War, in many different dimensions, was the most important and powerful single event in American history. Now that's saying a lot, because it means that it was more important, more powerful, in shaping this nation than the Revolution itself, which gave birth to the nation.

—JAMES McPHERSON (1943–   ), interview with Roger Mudd, in *Great Minds of History,* 1999

We are constantly thinking of the great war . . . which saved the Union . . . but it was a war that did a great deal more than that. It created in this country what had never existed before—a national consciousness. It was not the salvation of the Union, it was the rebirth of the Union.

—WOODROW WILSON (1856–1924), speech, May 31, 1915

Civilization

The whole history of civilization is strewn with creeds and institutions which were invaluable at first, and deadly afterward.

—WALTER BAGEHOT (1826–1877), *Physics and Politics,* 1872

Everything an Indian does is in a circle, and that is because the power of the world always works in circles and everything tries to be round. In the old days when we were a strong and happy people, all our power came to us from the sacred hoop of the nation, and so long as the hoop was unbroken the people flourished.

—BLACK ELK (1863–1950), in John G. Neihardt, *Black Elk Speaks,* 1961

A great civilization is not conquered from without until it has destroyed itself within.

—WILL DURANT (1885–1981), *Caesar and Christ,* 1944

Civilization is a stream with banks. The stream is sometimes filled with blood from people killing, stealing, shouting and doing the things historians usually record, while on the banks, unnoticed, people build homes, make love, raise children, sing songs, write poetry and even whittle statues. The story of civilization is the story of what happened on the banks. Historians are pessimists because they ignore the banks for the river.

— WILL DURANT (1885–1981), *Life*, October 18, 1963

Once more, in the great systole and diastole of history, an age of freedom ended and an age of discipline began.

— WILL DURANT (1885–1981), *Caesar and Christ*, 1944

Civilization is a process in the service of Eros, whose purpose is to combine single human individuals, and after that families, then races, peoples and nations, into one great unity, the unity of mankind. Why this has to happen, we do not know; the work of Eros is precisely this.

— SIGMUND FREUD (1856–1939), *Civilization and its Discontents*, 1931

[The Greeks] were the first Westerners; the spirit of the West, the modern spirit, is a Greek discovery and the place of the Greeks is in the modern world.

— EDITH HAMILTON (1867–1963), *The Greek Way*, 1930

Among the laws controlling human societies there is one more precise and clearer, it seems to me, than all the others. If men are to remain civilized or to become civilized, the art of association must develop and improve among them at the same speed as equality of conditions spreads.

— ALEXIS DE TOCQUEVILLE (1805–1859), *Democracy in America*, 1840

Civilization is a movement and not a condition, a voyage and not a harbor.

— A. J. TOYNBEE (1889–1975), in *The Reader's Digest*, October 1958

It is the historical function of civilizations to serve, by their down-falls, as stepping stones to a progressive process of the revelation of always deeper religious insight, and the gift of ever more grace to act on this insight.

⟶ A. J. TOYNBEE (1889–1975), *Christianity and Civilization*, 1947

If Germany, thanks to Hitler and his successors, were to enslave the European nations and destroy most of the treasures of their past, future historians would certainly pronounce that she had civilized Europe.

⟶ SIMONE WEIL (1909–1943), "The Great Beast," 1940, in *Notebooks*, 1956

 *Class and Caste*

The bonds of class are stronger than those of nationality.

⟶ LORD ACTON (1834–1902), "Political Causes of the American Revolution," in *Essays on Freedom and Power*, 1949

Real good breeding, as the people have it here, is one of the finest things now going in the world. The careful avoidance of all discussion, the swift hopping from topic to topic, does not agree with me; but the graceful style they do it with is beyond that of minuets!

⟶ THOMAS CARLYLE (1795–1881), letter, July 17, 1844, quoted in Fred Kaplan, *Thomas Carlyle: A Biography*, 1983

By bourgeoisie is meant the class of modern capitalists, owners of the means of social production and employers of wage labor. By proletariat, the class of modern wage laborers who, having no means of production of their own, are reduced to selling their labor power in order to live.

⟶ KARL MARX (1818–1883) and FRIEDRICH ENGELS (1820–1895), *The Communist Manifesto*, 1848

The danger is not that a particular class is unfit to govern. Every class is unfit to govern.
— LORD ACTON (1834–1902), letter, March 24, 1881

An aristocracy is a combination of many powerful men, for the purpose of maintaining and advancing their own particular interests.
— JAMES FENIMORE COOPER (1789–1851), *The American Democrat,* 1838

At the bottom, people tend to believe that class is defined by the amount of money you have. In the middle, people grant that money has something to do with it, but think education and the kind of work you do almost equally important. Near the top, people perceive that taste, values, ideas, style, and behavior are indispensable criteria of class, regardless of money or occupation or education.
— PAUL FUSSELL (1924–   ), *Class,* 1983

The history of all hitherto existing society is the history of class struggles.
— KARL MARX (1818–1883) and FRIEDRICH ENGELS (1820–1895), *The Communist Manifesto,* 1848

Beggars . . . should be entirely abolished! Truly, it is annoying to give to them and annoying not to give to them.
— FRIEDRICH NIETZSCHE (1844–1900), *Thus Spoke Zarathustra,* 1884

The Americans never use the word *peasant,* because they have no idea of the class which that term denotes; the ignorance of more remote ages, the simplicity of rural life, and the rusticity of the villager have not been preserved among them; and they are alike unacquainted with the virtues, the vices, the coarse habits, and the simple graces of an early stage of civilization.
— ALEXIS DE TOCQUEVILLE (1805–1859), *Democracy in America,* 1840

What is most important for democracy is not that great fortunes should not exist, but that great fortunes should not remain in the same hands. In that way there are rich men, but they do not form a class.

— ALEXIS DE TOCQUEVILLE (1805–1859), *Democracy in America,* 1840

 *Commerce*

Trade is the natural enemy of all violent passions. Trade loves moderation, delights in compromise, and is most careful to avoid anger. It is patient, supple, and insinuating, only resorting to extreme measures in cases of absolute necessity. Trade makes men independent of one another and gives them a high idea of their personal importance: it leads them to want to manage their own affairs and teaches them to succeed therein. Hence it makes them inclined to liberty but disinclined to revolution.

— ALEXIS DE TOCQUEVILLE (1805–1859), *Democracy in America,* 1840

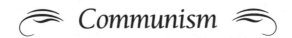 *Communism*

It wasn't idealism that made me, from the beginning, want a more secure and rational society. It was an intellectual judgement, to which I still hold. When I was young, its name was socialism. We can be deflected by names. But the need was absolute, and is still absolute.

— RAYMOND WILLIAMS (1921–1988), *Loyalties,* 1985

From Stettin in the Baltic to Trieste in the Adriatic, an iron curtain has descended across the Continent.

━ WINSTON CHURCHILL (1874–1965), speech to Westminster College, Fulton, Missouri, March 5, 1946

I have no concern with any economic criticisms of the communist system; I cannot enquire into whether the abolition of private property is expedient or advantageous. But I am able to recognize that the psychological premises on which the system is based are an untenable illusion. In abolishing private property we deprive the human love of aggression of one of its instruments . . . but we have in no way altered the differences in power and influence which are misused by aggressiveness.

━ SIGMUND FREUD (1856–1939), *Civilization and Its Discontents*, 1930

A specter is haunting Europe—the specter of communism.

━ KARL MARX (1818–1883) and FRIEDRICH ENGELS (1820–1895), *The Communist Manifesto*, 1848

In a higher phase of communist society . . . only then can the narrow horizon of bourgeois right be fully left behind and society inscribe on its banners: from each according to his ability, to each according to his needs.

━ KARL MARX (1818–1883), *Critique of the Gotha Program*, 1875

The theory of the Communists may be summed up in the single sentence: Abolition of private property.

━ KARL MARX (1818–1883) and FRIEDRICH ENGELS (1820–1895), *The Communist Manifesto*, 1848

The crusade against Communism was even more imaginary than the spectre of Communism.

━ A. J. P. TAYLOR (1906–1990), *The Origins of the Second World War*, 1961

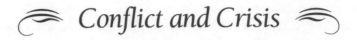

Conflict and Crisis

[Crises are] the acceleration of historical process.
— JACOB BURCKHARDT (1818–1897), *The Crises of History,* 1869

No man lives without jostling and being jostled; in all ways he has to elbow himself through the world, giving and receiving offence.
— THOMAS CARLYLE (1795–1881), *Critical and Miscellaneous Essays,* 1838

There cannot be a crisis next week. My schedule is already full.
— HENRY A. KISSINGER (1923–   ), quoted in conversation, *New York Times Magazine,* June 1, 1969

One often contradicts an opinion when what is uncongenial is really the tone in which it was conveyed.
— FRIEDRICH NIETZSCHE (1844–1900), *Human, All Too Human,* 1878

Extreme positions are not succeeded by moderate ones, but by *contrary* extreme positions.
— FRIEDRICH NIETZSCHE (1844–1900), *The Will to Power,* 1888

The man of knowledge must be able not only to love his enemies but also to hate his friends.
— FRIEDRICH NIETZSCHE (1844–1900), *Ecce Homo,* 1888

To knock a thing down, especially if it is cocked at an arrogant angle, is a deep delight to the blood.
— GEORGE SANTAYANA (1863–1952), *The Life of Reason,* 1905

When great causes are on the move in the world, stirring all men's souls, drawing them from their firesides, casting aside comfort, wealth, and the pursuit of happiness in response to impulses at once awe-striking and irresistible, we learn that we are spirits, not animals.
— WINSTON CHURCHILL (1874–1965), radio broadcast, June 16, 1941

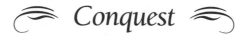 *Conquest*

It should be noted that when he seizes a state, the new ruler ought to determine all the injuries that he will need to inflict. He should inflict them once and for all, and not have to renew them every day.

➤ NICCOLÒ MACHIAVELLI (1469–1527), *The Prince*, 1514

Violence should be inflicted once and for all; people will then forget what it tastes like and so be less resentful.

➤ NICCOLÒ MACHIAVELLI (1469–1527), *The Prince*, 1514

 *Consequences*

The rebound is proportioned to the blow.

➤ JAMES FENIMORE COOPER (1789–1851), *The American Democrat*, 1838

Often an entire city has suffered because of an evil man.

➤ HESIOD (active 8th century B.C.), *Works and Days*

We all praise fidelity; but the true friend pays the penalty when he supports those whom Fortune crushes.

➤ LUCAN (39–65), *The Civil War*

Suppose . . . that Lenin had died of typhus in Siberia in 1895 and Hitler had been killed on the western front in 1916. What would the twentieth century have looked like now?

➤ ARTHUR SCHLESINGER, JR. (1917–   ), *The Cycles of American History*, 1986

In history an additional result is commonly produced by human actions beyond that which they aim at and obtain—that which they immediately recognize and desire. They gratify their own interest; but something further is thereby accomplished, latent in the actions in question, though not present to their consciousness, and not included in their design.

— GEORG HEGEL (1770–1831), *The Philosophy of History*, 1837

 *Courage*

The courage of a soldier is found to be the cheapest and most common quality of human nature.

— EDWARD GIBBON (1737–1794), *The Decline and Fall of the Roman Empire*, 1776–1788

Valor is of no service, chance rules all, and the bravest often fall by the hands of cowards.

— SNORRI STURLUSON (1179–1241), *Heimskringla*

Bravery is half victory.

— TACITUS (ca. 55–ca. 120), *The Histories*

But the bravest are surely those who have the clearest vision of what is before them, glory and danger alike, and yet notwithstanding go out to meet it.

— THUCYDIDES (ca. 460–400 B.C.), *The History of the Peloponnesian War*

Creativity and Imagination

Susceptibility to the highest forces is the highest genius.
— HENRY BROOK ADAMS (1838–1918), *The Education of Henry Adams,* 1907

Every animal leaves traces of what it was; man alone leaves traces of what he has created.
— JACOB BRONOWSKI (1908–1974), *The Ascent of Man,* 1973

A man cannot make a pair of shoes rightly unless he do it in a devout manner.
— THOMAS CARLYLE (1795–1881), letter, October 22, 1842

The world is a republic of mediocrities, and always was.
— THOMAS CARLYLE (1795–1881), letter, May 13, 1853

[Poets:] They raise their minds by brooding over and embellishing their sufferings, from one degree of fervid exaltation and dreary greatness to another, till at length they run amuck entirely, and whoever meets them would do well to run them thro' the body.
— THOMAS CARLYLE (1795–1881), letter, January 28, 1821

There is no logic to creative thought. Creativity makes its own rules. Genius transcends them. The aboriginal act of inspiration remains utterly mysterious to human understanding. We know when it happens, but not how or why.
— DAVID HACKETT FISCHER (1935–   ), *Historians' Fallacies: Toward a Logic of Historical Thought,* 1970

It has been said that there are two ways of manifesting an intellectual subservience to another mind: slavish imitation and obsessive refutation. Both of these forms of servility are regrettably common in historical scholarship.

— DAVID HACKETT FISCHER (1935–   ), *Historians' Fallacies: Toward a Logic of Historical Thought,* 1970

There really is no such thing as Art. There are only artists.

— E. H. GOMBRICH (1909–   ), *The Story of Art,* 1950

It is a matter of perfect indifference where a thing originated; the only question is: "Is it true in and for itself?"

— GEORG HEGEL (1770–1831), *The Philosophy of History,* 1837

Custom, then, is the great guide of human life.

— DAVID HUME (1711–1776), *An Enquiry Concerning Human Understanding,* 1748

In effect, the only tokens of history continually available to our sense are the desirable things made by men. Of course, to say that man-made things are desirable is redundant, because man's native inertia is overcome only by desire, and nothing gets made unless it is desirable.

— GEORGE KUBLER (1912–   ), *The Shape of Time: Remarks on the History of Things,* 1962

Although this has been called the age of anxiety, it might better be termed the century of the blues, after the moody song style that was born sometime around 1900 in the Mississippi Delta.

— ALAN LOMAX (1915–   ), *The Land Where the Blues Began,* 1993

[The poet and playwright John Dryden's] imagination resembled the wings of an ostrich. It enabled him to run, though not to soar.

— THOMAS BABINGTON MACAULAY (1800–1859), "On John Dryden," 1828, reprinted in *Critical and Historical Essays,* 1843

Men nearly always follow the tracks made by others and proceed in their affairs by imitation, even though they cannot entirely keep to the tracks of others or emulate the prowess of their models. So a prudent man should always follow in the footsteps of great men and imitate those who have been outstanding. If his own prowess fails to compare with theirs, at least it has an air of greatness about it. He should behave like those archers who, if they are skillful, when the target seems too distant, know the capabilities of their bow and aim a good deal higher than their objective, not in order to shoot so high but so that by aiming high they can reach the target.

➖ Niccolò Machiavelli (1469–1527), *The Prince,* 1514

There are three kinds of intelligence: one kind understands things for itself, the other appreciates what others can understand, the third understands neither for itself nor through others. This first kind is excellent, the second good, and the third kind useless.

➖ Niccolò Machiavelli (1469–1527), *The Prince,* 1514

On a level plain, simple mounds look like hills; and the insipid flatness of our present bourgeoisie is to be measured by the altitude of its "great intellects."

➖ Karl Marx (1818–1883), *Capital,* 1867

Perhaps no person can be a poet, or can even enjoy poetry, without a certain unsoundness of mind.

➖ Thomas Babington Macaulay (1800–1859), "Milton," 1825, reprinted in *Critical and Historical Essays,* 1843

He who, in an enlightened and literary society, aspires to be a great poet, must first become a little child. He must take to pieces the whole web of his mind. He must unlearn much of that knowledge which has perhaps constituted hitherto his chief title to superiority. His very talents will be a hindrance to him.

➖ Thomas Babington Macaulay (1800–1859), "Milton," 1825, reprinted in *Critical and Historical Essays,* 1843

As the unity of the modern world becomes increasingly a techno-logical rather than a social affair, the techniques of the arts provide the most valuable means of insight into the real direction of our own collective purposes.

— MARSHALL MCLUHAN (1911–1980), *The Mechanical Bride*, 1951

Most works of art are effectively treated as commodities and most artists, even when they justly claim quite other intentions, are effectively treated as a category of independent *craftsmen* or *skilled workers* producing a certain kind of marginal commodity.

— RAYMOND WILLIAMS (1921–1988), *Keywords*, 1976

Only the most acute and active animals are capable of boredom. A theme for a great poet would be *God's boredom* on the seventh day of creation.

— FRIEDRICH NIETZSCHE (1844–1900), *The Wanderer and His Shadow*, 1880

The desire to create continually is vulgar and betrays jealousy, envy, ambition. If one is something, one really does not need to make anything—and one nonetheless does very much. There exists above the "productive" man a yet higher species.

— FRIEDRICH NIETZSCHE (1844–1900), *Human, All Too Human*, 1878

Whatever its manner of expression, popular culture and the arts included in that culture can no longer be treated with contempt or dismissed as unworthy of study. . . . To erase the boundaries, cre-ated by snobbery and cultism, that have so long divided the arts means, in the long run, greater understanding of them.

— RUSSEL NYE (1913–   ), *The Unembarrassed Muse: The Popular Arts in America*, 1970

Every intellectual product must be judged from the point of view of the age and the people in which it was produced.

— WALTER PATER (1839–1894), *Studies in the History of the Renais-sance*, 1873

Against boredom the gods themselves fight in vain.
— FRIEDRICH NIETZSCHE (1844–1900), *The Anti-Christ*, 1895

To burn always with this hard, gemlike flame, to maintain this ecstasy, is success in life.
— WALTER PATER (1839–1894), *Studies in the History of the Renaissance*, 1873

The poet is in command of his fantasy, while it is exactly the mark of the neurotic that he is possessed by his fantasy.
— LIONEL TRILLING (1905–1976), *The Liberal Imagination*, 1950

The poet . . . may be used as the barometer, but let us not forget that he is also part of the weather.
— LIONEL TRILLING (1905–1976), *The Liberal Imagination*, 1950

Methodology can only bring us reflective understanding of the means which have demonstrated their value in practice by raising them to the level of explicit consciousness; it is no more the precondition of fruitful intellectual work than the knowledge of anatomy is a precondition for "correct" walking. Indeed, just as a person who attempted to govern his mode of walking continuously by anatomical knowledge would be in danger of stumbling, so the professional scholar who attempted to determine the aims of his own research extrinsically on the basis of methodological reflections would be in danger of falling into the same difficulties.
— MAX WEBER (1864–1920), *The Methodology of the Social Sciences*, 1949

 *Crime and Corruption*

The world of crime . . . is a last refuge of the authentic, uncorrupted, spontaneous event.
— DANIEL J. BOORSTIN (1914–   ), *The Image: A Guide to Pseudo-Events in America*, 1961

Corruption, the most infallible symptom of constitutional liberty.

— EDWARD GIBBON (1737–1794), *The Decline and Fall of the Roman Empire,* (1776–1788)

Nothing is quite so wretchedly corrupt as an aristocracy which has lost its power but kept its wealth and which still has endless leisure to devote to nothing but banal enjoyments. All its great thoughts and passionate energy are things of the past, and nothing but a host of petty, gnawing vices now cling to it like worms to a corpse.

— ALEXIS DE TOCQUEVILLE (1805–1859), *Democracy in America,* 1840

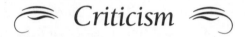 *Criticism*

We have our little *theory* on all human and divine things. Poetry, the workings of genius itself, which, in all times, with one or another meaning, has been called Inspiration, and held to be mysterious and inscrutable, is no longer without its scientific exposition. The building of the lofty rhyme is like any other masonry or bricklaying: we have theories of its rise, height, decline and fall—which latter, it would seem, is now near, among all people.

— THOMAS CARLYLE (1795–1881), "Signs of the Times," 1829, reprinted in *Critical and Miscellaneous Essays,* 1838

The author himself is the best judge of his own performance; none has so deeply meditated on the subject; none is so sincerely interested in the event.

— EDWARD GIBBON (1737–1794), *Memoirs of My Life,* 1796

It is easier to discover a deficiency in individuals, in states, and in Providence, than to see their real import and value.

— GEORG HEGEL (1770–1831), *The Philosophy of History,* 1837

Nothing is beautiful, only man: on this piece of naivete rests all aesthetics; it is the *first* truth of aesthetics. Let us immediately add its second: nothing is ugly but *degenerate* man—the domain of aesthetic judgment is therewith defined.

— FRIEDRICH NIETZSCHE (1844–1900), *Twilight of the Idols*, 1889

Culture and Society

Our attitude toward our own culture has recently been characterized by two qualities, braggadocio and petulance. Braggadocio— empty boasting of American power, American virtue, American know-how—has dominated our foreign relations now for some decades. . . . Here at home—within the family, so to speak—our attitude to our culture expresses a superficially different spirit, the spirit of petulance. Never before, perhaps, has a culture been so fragmented into groups, each full of its own virtue, each annoyed and irritated at the others.

— DANIEL J. BOORSTIN (1914–   ), *America and the Image of Europe*, 1960

The bourgeoisie . . . has been the first to show what man's activity can bring about. It has accomplished wonders far surpassing Egyptian pyramids, Roman aqueducts and Gothic cathedrals. . . . The bourgeoisie . . . draws all, even the most barbarian nations, into civilization. . . . It has created enormous cities . . . and has thus rescued a considerable part of the population from the idiocy of rural life. . . . The bourgeoisie, during its rule of scarce one hundred years, has created more massive and more colossal productive forces than have all preceding generations together.

— KARL MARX (1818–1883) and FRIEDRICH ENGELS (1820–1895), *The Communist Manifesto*, 1848

Society does not consist of individuals but expresses the sum of interrelations, the relations within which these individuals stand.
— KARL MARX (1818–1883), *Grundrisse,* written 1857–1858; published 1939

We call it a Society; and go about professing openly the totalest separation, isolation. Our life is not a mutual helpfulness; but rather, cloaked under due laws-of-war, named "fair competition" and so forth, it is a mutual hostility.
— THOMAS CARLYLE (1795–1881), *Past and Present,* 1843

The bourgeoisie of the whole world, which looks complacently upon the wholesale massacre after the battle, is convulsed by horror at the desecration of brick and mortar.
— KARL MARX (1818–1883), Address to the General Council of the International Working Men's Association, 1871, published in *Selected Works,* 1942

It is always possible to bind together a considerable number of people in love, so long as there are other people left over to receive the manifestations of their aggression.
— SIGMUND FREUD (1856–1939), *Civilization and Its Discontents,* 1930

The ideas of the ruling class are in every epoch the ruling ideas, i.e., the class which is the ruling *material* force of society is at the same time its ruling *intellectual* force.
— KARL MARX (1818–1883) and FRIEDRICH ENGELS (1820–1895), *The German Ideology,* 1846

[Organization men] are the ones of our middle class who have left home, spiritually as well as physically, to take the vows of organization life, and it is they who are the mind and soul of our great self-perpetuating institutions.
— WILLIAM WHYTE, JR. (1917–   ), *The Organization Man,* 1956

 *Curiosity*

The significance of man is that he is that part of the universe that asks the question, What is the significance of Man?
— CARL BECKER (1873–1945), *Progress and Power,* 1935

The American experience stirred mankind from *discovery* to *exploration.* From the cautious quest for what they knew (or thought they knew) was out there, into an enthusiastic reaching to the unknown. These are two substantially different kinds of human enterprise.
— DANIEL J. BOORSTIN (1914–   ), Reith Lecture, 1975, published
in *The Exploring Spirit: America and the World Experience,* 1976

That is the essence of science: ask an impertinent question, and you are on the way to a pertinent answer.
— JACOB BRONOWSKI (1908–1974), *The Ascent of Man,* 1973

Disinterested intellectual curiosity is the life blood of real civilisation.
— G. M. TREVELYAN (1876–1962), *English Social History,* 1942

 *Deceit and Deception*

We begin by fooling others and end up fooling ourselves.
— ERIC ALTERMAN (1960–   ), *Sound and Fury: The Washington
Punditocracy and the Collapse of American Politics,* 1992

The hypocrite's crime is that he bears false witness against himself.
— HANNAH ARENDT (1906–1975), *On Revolution,* 1963

We [twentieth-century Americans] risk being the first people in history to have been able to make their illusions so vivid, so persuasive, so "realistic" that they can live in them. We are the most illusioned people on earth.

— DANIEL J. BOORSTIN (1914–), *The Image: A Guide to Pseudo-Events in America,* 1961

A deft administrator these days must master "the technique of denying the truth without actually lying."

— DANIEL J. BOORSTIN (1914–), *The Image: A Guide to Pseudo-Events in America,* 1961

"Truth" has been displaced by "believability" as the test of the statements which dominate our lives.

— DANIEL J. BOORSTIN (1914–), *The Image: A Guide to Pseudo-Events in America,* 1961

A man calumniated is doubly injured—first by him who utters the calumny, and then by him who believes it.

— HERODOTUS (ca. 484–ca. 425 B.C.), *Histories,* ca. 430 B.C.

Most marks [suckers] come from the upper strata of society, which, in America, means that they have made, married, or inherited money. Because of this, they acquire status which in time they come to attribute to some inherent superiority, especially as regards matters of sound judgment in finance and investment. Friends and associates, themselves social climbers and sycophants, help to maintain this illusion of superiority. Eventually, the mark comes to regard himself as a person of vision and even a genius. Thus a Babbitt who has cleared half a million in a real-estate development easily forgets the part which luck and chicanery have played in his financial rise; he accepts his mantle of respectability without question; he naively attributes his success to sound business judgment. And any confidence man will testify that a real-estate man is the fattest and juiciest of suckers.

— DAVID MAURER (1906–1981), *The Big Con,* 1940

Always sensitive to any change in the east, Hitler's suspicions of the Russians mounted in proportion to the treachery of his own intentions.

— ALAN BULLOCK (1914–   ), *Hitler: A Study in Tyranny*, 1953

Ambition drove many men to become false; to have one thought locked in the breast, another ready on the tongue.

— SALLUST (86–34 B.C.), *The War with Cataline*

[Men] use thought only to justify their injustices, and speech only to disguise their thoughts.

— VOLTAIRE (1694–1778), *Dialogues*, 1765

 *Decisions*

Nothing is inevitable in life. That's my most basic position as historian: People make choices, and those choices have results, and we all live with the results.

— STEPHEN AMBROSE (1936–   ), interview with Roger Mudd, in *Great Minds of History*, 1999

[Upon crossing the Rubicon:] The die is cast.

— JULIUS CAESAR (100–44 B.C.), quoting a proverb

Great deeds are usually wrought at great risks.

— HERODOTUS (ca. 484–after 424 B.C.), *The Histories*

Human actions are not the mechanical effects of causes; they are purposive executions of decisions between alternative possible choices.

— A. J. TOYNBEE (1889–1975), *A Study of History*, 1961

Drawing his sword, [Pizarro] traced a line with it on the sand from East to West. Then, turning towards the South, "Friends and comrades!" he said, "on that side are toil, hunger, nakedness, the drenching storm, desertion, and death; on this side ease and pleasure. There lies Peru with its riches; here, Panama and its poverty. Choose, each man, what best becomes a brave Castilian. For my part, go to the South." So saying, he stepped across the line.

    — WILLIAM HICKLING PRESCOTT (1796–1859), *The Conquest of Peru,* 1847

We human beings do have some genuine freedom of choice and therefore some effective control over our own destinies. I am not a determinist. But I also believe that the decisive choice is seldom the latest choice in the series. More often than not, it will turn out to be some choice made relatively far back in the past.

    — A. J. TOYNBEE (1889–1975), "Some Great 'If's' of History," *The New York Times,* March 5, 1961

 *Democracy*

At no time, at no place, in solemn convention assembled, through no chosen agents, had the American people officially proclaimed the United States to be a democracy. The Constitution did not contain the word. . . . When the Constitution was framed, no respectable person called himself or herself a democrat.

    — CHARLES AUSTIN BEARD (1874–1948) and MARY RITTER BEARD (1876–1958), *America in Midpassage,* 1939

The doctrine of equality! . . . There exists no more poisonous poison: for it *seems* to be preached by justice itself, while it is the *end* of justice.

    — FRIEDRICH NIETZSCHE (1844–1900), *Twilight of the Idols,* 1889

Democracy inevitably takes the tone of the lower portions of society, and, if there are great diversities, degrades the higher. Slavery is the only protection that has ever been known against this tendency, and it is so far true that slavery is essential to democracy. For where there are great incongruities in the constitution of society, if the American were to admit the Indians, the Chinese, the Negroes, to the rights to which they are justly jealous of admitting European emigrants, the country would be thrown into disorder, and if not, would be degraded to the level of barbarous races. . . . This is a good argument . . . , in the interest of all parties, against the emancipation of the blacks.

    — LORD ACTON (1834–1902), "Political Causes of the American Revolution," 1861, in *Essays on Freedom and Power*, 1948

Reborn from ancient Greece, democracy entered the twentieth century as a boisterous but lonely young orphan, and stands now after a blip of time as a solitary grandparent, somewhat listless in triumph, with scarcely anyone on the planet arguing for the future of a rival or descendant political order.

    — TAYLOR BRANCH, "Freedom Ascendant: The Challenge of Democracy," in Lorraine Glennon, ed., *Our Times: The Illustrated History of the 20th Century*, 1995

People think they have taken quite an extraordinarily bold step forward when they have rid themselves of belief in hereditary monarchy and swear by the democratic republic. In reality, however, the state is nothing but a machine for the oppression of one class by another, and indeed in the democratic republic no less than in the monarchy.

    — FRIEDRICH ENGELS (1820–1895), Introduction to 1891 edition of Karl Marx's *The Civil War in France*

Democracy is clearly most appropriate for countries which enjoy an economic surplus and least appropriate for countries where there is an economic insufficiency.

    — DAVID POTTER (1910–1971), *People of Plenty: Abundance and the American Character*, 1954

In democratic ages men rarely sacrifice themselves for another, but they show a general compassion for all the human race. One never sees them inflict pointless suffering, and they are glad to relieve the sorrows of others when they can do so without much trouble to themselves. They are not disinterested, but they are gentle.

➤ ALEXIS DE TOCQUEVILLE (1805–1859), *Democracy in America,* 1840

However energetically society in general may strive to make all the citizens equal and alike, the personal pride of each individual will always make him try to escape from the common level, and he will form some inequality somewhere to his own profit.

➤ ALEXIS DE TOCQUEVILLE (1805–1859), *Democracy in America,* 1840

Not only does democracy make every man forget his ancestors, but also clouds their view of their descendants and isolates them from their contemporaries. Each man is forever thrown back on himself alone, and there is danger that he may be shut up in the solitude of his own heart.

➤ ALEXIS DE TOCQUEVILLE (1805–1859), *Democracy in America,* 1840

In other words, a democratic government is the only one in which those who vote for a tax can escape the obligation to pay it.

➤ ALEXIS DE TOCQUEVILLE (1805–1859), *Democracy in America,* 1840

Democracy is not so much a form of government as a set of principles.

➤ WOODROW WILSON (1856–1924), *Atlantic Monthly,* March 1901

That a peasant may become king does not render the kingdom democratic.

➤ WOODROW WILSON (1856–1924), speech, August 31, 1910

 *Discontent*

No sooner is your ocean filled, than he grumbles that it might have been of better vintage. Try him with half of a Universe, of an Omnipotence, he sets to quarrelling with the proprietor of the other half, and declares himself the most maltreated of men. Always there is a black spot in our sunshine: it is even as I said, the *Shadow of Ourselves*.

— THOMAS CARLYLE (1795–1881), *Sartor Resartus,* 1834

Men think to mend their condition by a change of circumstances. They might as well hope to escape from their shadows.

— JAMES A. FROUDE (1818–1894), *Thomas Carlyle: A History of His First Forty Years,* 1882

 *Economics*

Capital is dead labor, which, vampire-like, lives only by sucking living labor, and lives the more, the more labor it sucks.

— KARL MARX (1818–1883), *Capital,* 1867

Capital is money, capital is commodities. . . . By virtue of it being value, it has acquired the occult ability to add value to itself. It brings forth living offspring, or, at the least, lays golden eggs.

— KARL MARX (1818–1883), *Capital,* 1867

Conspicuous consumption of valuable goods is a means of reputability to the gentleman of leisure.

— THORSTEIN VEBLEN (1857–1929), *The Theory of the Leisure Class,* 1899

In a society of abundance, the productive capacity can supply new kinds of goods faster than society in the mass learns to crave these goods or to regard them as necessities. If this new capacity is to be used, the imperative must fall upon consumption, and the society must be adjusted to a new set of drives and values in which consumption is paramount.

— DAVID POTTER (1910–1971), *People of Plenty: Economic Abundance and the American Character*, 1954

 *Education*

A teacher affects eternity; he can never tell where his influence stops.

— HENRY BROOK ADAMS (1838–1918), *The Education of Henry Adams*, 1907

They know enough who know how to learn.

— HENRY BROOK ADAMS (1838–1918), *The Education of Henry Adams*, 1907

Education is the art of making man ethical.

— GEORG HEGEL (1770–1831), *The Philosophy of Right*, 1821

It's as if something is eating away at the national memory. And, believe me, it's real. What students at good universities and good colleges today don't know about basic American history is appalling.

— DAVID McCULLOUGH (1933–   ), interview with Roger Mudd, in *Great Minds of History*, 1999

The very spring and root of honesty and virtue lie in good education.

— PLUTARCH (before 50–after 120), *Morals*

[On the reading habits of frontier Americans:] There is hardly a pioneer's hut which does not contain a few odd volumes of Shakespeare. I remember reading the feudal drama of *Henry V* for the first time in a log cabin.
    —ALEXIS DE TOCQUEVILLE (1805–1859), *Democracy in America,* 1840

Socrates gave no diplomas or degrees, and would have subjected any disciple who demanded one to a disconcerting catechism on the nature of true knowledge.
    —G. M. TREVELYAN (1876–1962), *History of England,* 1926

Enemies

To the extent that both Indian and white have denied one another their humanity, then to that extent both have demeaned democracy and the republican ideal. To the extent that hatred and war have prevailed, to that extent we have belittled the ideals and concepts of the Founding Fathers—and demeaned our own humanity. Every blow, physical and verbal, red and white, has diminished us and damaged the fabric of ourselves.
    —ODIE B. FAULK (1933–   ), *Crimson Desert: Indian Wars of the American Southwest,* 1974

You may have enemies whom you hate, but not enemies whom you despise. You must be proud of your enemy: then the success of your enemy shall be your success too.
    —FRIEDRICH NIETZSCHE (1844–1900), *Thus Spoke Zarathustra,* 1884

I have only ever made one prayer to God, a very short one: "O Lord, make my enemies ridiculous." And God granted it.
    —VOLTAIRE (1694–1778), letter, May 16, 1767

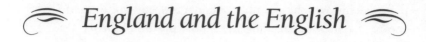 *England and the English*

[London:] That monstrous tuberosity of civilised life, the capital of England.
— THOMAS CARLYLE (1795–1881), *Sartor Resartus,* 1834

An acre in Middlesex is better than a principality in Utopia.
— THOMAS BABINGTON MACAULAY (1800–1859), "Lord Bacon," 1837, reprinted in *Critical and Historical Essays,* 1843

The English have all the material requisites for the revolution. What they lack is the spirit of generalization and revolutionary ardour.
— KARL MARX (1818–1883), pamphlet against the Bakuninists, 1870

The English are the nation of consummate cant.
— FRIEDRICH NIETZSCHE (1844–1900), *Twilight of the Idols,* 1889

Who the first inhabitants of Britain were, whether natives or immigrants, remains obscure; one must remember we are dealing with barbarians.
— TACITUS (ca. 55–ca. 120), *Agricola*

 *Events*

From time to time a great event, ardently desired, does not take place because some future time will fulfill it in greater perfection.
— JACOB BURCKHARDT (1818–1897), "On Fortune and Misfortune in History," 1871, in *Judgements on History and Historians,* 1958

It was one of those events which are incredible until they happen.
  ━ WINSTON CHURCHILL (1874–1965), *Great Contemporaries*, 1937

In retrospect, all events seem inevitable.
  ━ HENRY A. KISSINGER (1923–   ), *The White House Years*, 1979

Nearly every historical event is simultaneously an act of "securing" by somebody of the already ripened fruit of preceding development and a link in the chain of events which are preparing the fruits for the future.
  ━ GEORGE PLEKHANOV (1856–1918?), *The Role of the Individual in History*, 1898

Historical events are not inevitable; it's only in retrospect that they seem so.
  ━ A. J. TOYNBEE (1889–1975), quoted in Philip Toynbee, *Comparing Notes: A Dialogue Across a Generation*, 1963

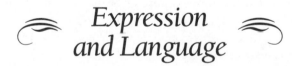 *Expression and Language*

There is a great discovery still to be made in literature, that of paying literary men by the quantity they *do not* write.
  ━ THOMAS CARLYLE (1795–1881), *London and Westminster Review* November 12, 1838; reprinted in *Critical and Miscellaneous Essays*, 1839

For, if a "good speaker," never so eloquent, does not see into the fact, and is not speaking the truth of that   is there a more horrid kind of object in creation?
  ━ THOMAS CARLYLE (1795–1881), "Inaugural Address at Edinburgh," 1866, published in *Scottish and Other Miscellanies*, 1915

It was observed by that remarkable twelfth-century chronicler, Henry of Huntington, that an interest in his past was one of the distinguishing characteristics of man as compared with the other animals. And in these days when the cultivated man or woman is conscious of deficiencies in his education without some knowledge of economics, medieval history, recent advances in the basic natural sciences, so also he may discover a desire to know something of the nature and development of his mother tongue. The medium by which he communicates his thought and feelings to his fellow man, the tool with which he conducts his business or the government of millions of people, the vehicle by which have been transmitted to him the science, the philosophy, the poetry of the race is surely worthy of study.

➤ ALBERT C. BAUGH (1891–1981), *A History of the English Language*, 1935

The most refined skills of color printing, the intricate techniques of wide-angle photography, provide us pictures of trivia bigger and more real than life. We forget that we see trivia and notice only that the reproduction is so good. Man fulfills his dream and by photographic magic produces a precise image of the Grand Canyon. The result is not that he adores nature or beauty the more. Instead he adores his camera—and himself.

➤ DANIEL J. BOORSTIN (1914–   ), *The Image: A Guide to Pseudo-Events in America*, 1961

Sarcasm I now see to be, in general, the language of the Devil; for which reason I have long since as good as renounced it.

➤ THOMAS CARLYLE (1795–1881), *Sartor Resartus*, 1834

Under all speech that is good for anything there lies a silence that is better. Silence is deep as Eternity; speech is shallow as Time.

➤ THOMAS CARLYLE (1795–1881), "Sir Walter Scott," 1838, reprinted in *Critical and Miscellaneous Essays*, 1839

Style is the image of character.

➤ EDWARD GIBBON (1737–1794), *Memoirs of My Life*, 1796

Writing is a dreadful Labour, yet not so dreadful as Idleness.
> ➤ THOMAS CARLYLE (1795–1881), *Two Notebooks of Thomas Carlyle*,
> 1898

In a symbol there is concealment and yet revelation: here therefore, by silence and by speech acting together, comes a double significance. . . . In the symbol proper, what we can call a symbol, there is ever, more or less distinctly and directly, some embodiment and revelation of the Infinite; the Infinite is made to blend itself with the Finite, to stand visible, and as it were, attainable there. By symbols, accordingly, is man guided and commanded, made happy, made wretched.
> ➤ THOMAS CARLYLE (1795–1881), *Sartor Resartus*, 1834

I pass with relief from the tossing sea of Cause and Theory to the firm ground of Result and Fact.
> ➤ WINSTON CHURCHILL (1874–1965), *The Malakand Field Force*,
> 1898

The style of an author should be the image of his mind, but the choice and command of language is the fruit of exercise.
> ➤ EDWARD GIBBON (1737–1794), *Memoirs of My Life*, 1796

It has always been my practice to cast a long paragraph in a single mould, to try it by my ear, to deposit it in my memory, but to suspend the action of the pen till I had given the last polish to my work.
> ➤ EDWARD GIBBON (1737–1794), *Memoirs of My Life*, 1796

[Francis Bacon] had a wonderful talent for packing thought close, and rendering it portable.
> ➤ THOMAS BABINGTON MACAULAY (1800–1859), "Lord Bacon," 1837,
> reprinted in *Lord Macaulay's Essays*, 1889

The writer may very well serve a movement of history as its mouthpiece, but he cannot of course create it.
> ➤ KARL MARX (1818–1883), *Moralizing Criticism and Critical*
> *Morality*, 1847

Language, the machine of the poet, is best fitted for his purpose in its rudest state. Nations, like individuals, first perceive, and then abstract. They advance from particular images to general terms. Hence the vocabulary of an enlightened society is philosophical, that of a half-civilised people is poetical.

— THOMAS BABINGTON MACAULAY (1800–1859), "Milton," 1825, reprinted in *Critical and Historical Essays,* 1843

An American cannot converse, but he can discuss, and his talk falls into a dissertation. He speaks to you as if he was addressing a meeting; and if he should chance to become warm in the discussion, he will say "Gentlemen" to the person with whom he is conversing.

— ALEXIS DE TOCQUEVILLE (1805–1859), *Democracy in America,* 1835–1840

The English Bible—a book which, if everything else in our language should perish, would alone suffice to show the whole extent of its beauty and power.

— THOMAS BABINGTON MACAULAY (1800–1859), "On John Dryden," 1828, reprinted in *Critical and Historical Essays,* 1843

Today it is not the classroom nor the classics which are the repositories of models of eloquence, but the ad agencies.

— MARSHALL MCLUHAN (1911–1980), *The Mechanical Bride,* 1951

In the mountains the shortest route is from peak to peak, but for that you must have long legs. Aphorisms should be peaks: and those to whom they are spoken should be big and tall of stature.

— FRIEDRICH NIETZSCHE (1844–1900), *Thus Spoke Zarathustra,* 1884

The aphorism, the apophthegm, in which I am the first master among Germans, are the forms of "eternity"; my ambition is to say in ten sentences what everyone else says in a book—what everyone else *does not* say in a book.

— FRIEDRICH NIETZSCHE (1844–1900), *Twilight of the Idols,* 1889

The object of oratory alone is not truth, but persuasion.
— THOMAS BABINGTON MACAULAY (1800–1859), "Essay on Athenian
Orators," in *The Works of Lord Macaulay,* 1898

A letter is an unannounced visit, the postman the agent of rude
surprises. One ought to reserve an hour a week for receiving letters
and afterwards take a bath.
— FRIEDRICH NIETZSCHE (1844–1900), *The Wanderer and His
Shadow,* 1880

The significance of language for the evolution of culture lies in
this, that mankind set up in language a separate world beside the
other world, a place it took to be so firmly set that, standing upon
it, it could lift the rest of the world off its hinges and make itself
master of it. To the extent that man has for long ages believed in
the concepts and names of things as in *aeternae veritates,* he has
appropriated to himself that pride by which he raised himself
above the animal: he really thought that in language he possessed
knowledge of the world.
— FRIEDRICH NIETZSCHE (1844–1900), *Human, All Too Human,* 1878

Speak softly and carry a big stick.
— THEODORE ROOSEVELT (1858–1919) speech, September 2, 1901

By and large the literature of a democracy will never exhibit the
order, regularity, skill, and art characteristic of aristocratic literature; formal qualities will be neglected or actually despised. The
style will often be strange, incorrect, overburdened, and loose, and
almost always strong and bold. Writers will be more anxious to
work quickly than to perfect details. Short works will be com-
moner than long books, wit than erudition, imagination than
depth. There will be a rude and untutored vigor of thought with
great variety and singular fecundity Authors will strive to astonish
more than to please, and to stir passions rather than to charm taste.
— ALEXIS DE TOCQUEVILLE (1805–1859), *Democracy in America,*
1835–1840

The genius of democracies is seen not only in the great number of new words introduced but even more in the new ideas they express.

— ALEXIS DE TOCQUEVILLE (1805–1859), *Democracy in America,* 1835–1840

Write regularly, day in and day out, at whatever times of day you find you write best. Don't wait till you feel that you are in the mood.

— A. J. TOYNBEE (1889–1975), *Experiences,* 1969

 *Fad and Fashion*

The star is the ultimate American verification of Jean-Jacques Rousseau's *Emile.* His mere existence proves the perfectability of any man or woman. Oh wonderful pliability of human nature, in a society where anyone can become a celebrity! And where any celebrity . . . may become a star!

— DANIEL J. BOORSTIN (1914–   ), *The Image: A Guide to Pseudo-Events in America,* 1961

If one considers how much reason every person has for anxiety and timid self-concealment, and how three-quarters of his energy and goodwill can be paralyzed and made unfruitful by it, one has to be very grateful to fashion, insofar as it sets that three-quarters free and communicates self-confidence and mutual cheerful agreeableness to those who know they are subject to its law.

— FRIEDRICH NIETZSCHE (1844–1900), *Human, All Too Human,* 1879

⸝ *Favors and Patronage* ⸜

Benefits should be conferred gradually; and in that way they will taste better.
— NICCOLÒ MACHIAVELLI (1469–1527), *The Prince*, 1514

⸝ *Folklore and Myth* ⸜

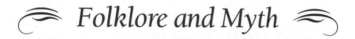

Myth is the secret opening through which the inexhaustible energies of the cosmos pour into human cultural manifestation.
— JOSEPH CAMPBELL (1904–1987), *The Hero with a Thousand Faces*, 1949

In spite of the accelerated pace of modern living, which seems to strike at our roots and very identity, the folklorist marvels at the tenacity of tradition. Veer off the main highway for a little distance, and the civilization of rocket ships and automation suddenly melts away. . . . The idea that folklore is dying out is itself a kind of folklore.
— RICHARD M. DORSON (1916–1981), *American Folklore*, 1959

The fact that men and women still do rise in the American world attests to the continued validity of [Horatio] Alger's belief in social mobility. . . . More obsolete than the Model T, Alger continues to be our mythmaker; until we show some of the same sort of ruthlessness about discarding outworn mythologies as we do about outdated motorcars, we shall never be able to get at the unprece dented meaning of American civilization today.
— KENNETH S. LYNN (1923–   ), *The Dream of Success: A Study of the Modern American Imagination*, 1955

[The Dutch settlers of New Netherland (New York)] claim to be the first inventors of those recondite beverages, cocktail, stone-fence, and sherry cobbler.

━━ WASHINGTON IRVING (1783–1859), *Knickerbocker's History of New York,* 1809

Having feasted [Captain John Smith] after their best barbarous manner they could, a long consultation was held, but the conclusion was, two great stones were brought before Powhatan: then as many as could layd hands on him, dragged him to them, and thereon laid his head, and being ready with their clubs, to beate out his braines, Pocahontas the Kings dearest daughter, when no intreaty could prevaile, got his head in her armes, and laid her owne upon his to save him from death: whereat the Emperour was contented he should live to make him hatchets, and her bells, beads, and copper . . .

━━ CAPTAIN JOHN SMITH (ca. 1580–1631), *The Generall Historie of Virginia, New-England, and the Summer Isles,* 1624

I can't tell a lie. I did cut [the cherry tree] with my hatchet.

━━ MASON LOCKE WEEMS (1759–1825), quotation attributed to George Washington as a child, in *The Life of George Washington,* 1800

The log cabin, the wagon train—these are things that when you see them now, stories pour out of them. They're used so widely in advertising, political campaigns, and other things. All you do is show the picture of the wagon train, and you know that here's a story of brave migrants setting off into the unknown, taking their destiny in their hands. Where you see a picture of the log cabin, here is somebody setting off in the middle of the wilderness with only their own resources to set up their life, and this is the small beginnings from which great things will flow. Those are icons, those are things that still resonate with, meaning for the American people.

━━ RICHARD WHITE (1947–   ), interview with Roger Mudd, in *Great Minds of History,* 1999

Whoso pulleth out this sword of this stone and anvil, is rightwise king born of all England.

— Sir Thomas Mallory (?–1471), *Le Morte d'Arthure*, 1485

The mythology of a nation is the intelligible mask of that enigma called the "national character."

— Richard Slotkin (1942–   ), *Regeneration Through Violence: The Mythology of the American Frontier, 1600–1860*, 1973

You can't understand history without understanding myths, because people don't mold their lives according to what actually happened. They mold their lives according to what they think happened. And what they think happened is encapsulated in myths.

— Richard White (1947–   ), interview with Roger Mudd, in *Great Minds of History*, 1999

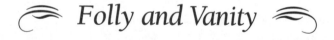

Folly and Vanity

Dedicated to human history: A dark and turbulent stream of folly, illuminated now and then by flashes of genius.

— Isaac Asimov (1920–1992), dedication page of *Asimov's Chronology of the World*, 1991

I fear animals regard man as a creature of their own kind which has in a highly dangerous fashion lost its healthy animal reason—as the mad animal, as the laughing animal, as the weeping animal, as the unhappy animal.

— Friedrich Nietzsche (1844–1900), *The Gay Science*, 1887

The greatest of faults, I should say, is to be conscious of none.

— Thomas Carlyle (1795–1881), *Heroes and Hero-Worship*, 1841

As individuals and as a nation, we now suffer from social narcissism. The beloved Echo of our ancestors, the virgin America, has been abandoned. We have fallen in love with our own image, with images of our making, which turn out to be images of ourselves.
— DANIEL J. BOORSTIN (1914–   ), *The Image: A Guide to Pseudo-Events in America,* 1961

Fancy that thou deservest to be hanged . . . thou wilt feel it happiness to be only shot: fancy that thou deservest to be hanged in a hair halter, it will be a luxury to die in hemp.
— THOMAS CARLYLE (1795–1881), *Sartor Resartus,* 1836

I would much rather have men ask why I have no statue than why I have one.
— THE ELDER CATO (234–149 B.C.), quoted in Plutarch, *Parallel Lives*

I understand by this passion the union of desire, friendship, and tenderness, which is inflamed by a single female, which prefers her to the rest of her sex, and which seeks her possession as the supreme or the sole happiness of our being.
— EDWARD GIBBON (1737–1794), *Memoirs of My Life,* 1796

We can endure neither our evils nor their cures.
— LIVY (59 B.C.–A.D. 17), *History*

[Title of book on the sinking of the *Titanic:*] A Night to Remember
— WALTER LORD (1917–   ), *A Night to Remember,* 1955

A commodity appears at first sight an extremely obvious, trivial thing. But its analysis brings out that it is a very strange thing, abounding in metaphysical subtleties and theological niceties.
— KARL MARX (1818–1883), *Capital,* 1867

In the United States today, opiates are the religion of the people.
— THOMAS SZASZ (1920–   ), *The Second Sin,* 1973

Give us the luxuries of life, and we will dispense with its necessaries.

➤ J. L. MOTLEY (1814–1877), quoted in Oliver Wendell Holmes, Sr., *The Autocrat of the Breakfast Table*, 1858

What is the vanity of the vainest man compared with the vanity which the most modest possesses when, in the midst of nature and the world, he feels himself to be "man"!

➤ FRIEDRICH NIETZSCHE (1844–1900), *The Wanderer and His Shadow*, 1880

If we do not find anything very pleasant, at least we shall find something new.

➤ VOLTAIRE (1694–1778), *Candide*, 1759

A Roman divorced from his wife, being highly blamed by his friends, who demanded, "Was she not chaste? Was she not fair? Was she not fruitful?" holding out his shoe, asked them whether it was not new and well made. "Yet," added he, "none of you can tell where it pinches me."

➤ PLUTARCH (before 50–after 120), "Aemilius Paulus," in *Parallel Lives*

Wooden-headedness consists of assessing a situation in terms of preconceived, fixed notions while ignoring or rejecting any contrary signs. It is acting according to wish while not allowing oneself to be confused by the facts.

➤ BARBARA TUCHMAN (1912–1989), "An Inquiry into the Persistence of Unwisdom in Government," *Esquire*, 1980

Consider any individual at any period of his life, and you will always find him preoccupied with fresh plans to increase his comfort. Do not talk to him about the interests and rights of the human race; that little private business of his for the moment absorbs all his thoughts, and he hopes that public disturbances can be put off to some other time.

➤ ALEXIS DE TOCQUEVILLE (1805–1859), *Democracy in America*, 1840

They named it *ovation* from the Latin *ovis* [a sheep].

— PLUTARCH (before 50–after 120), "Marcellus," *in Parallel Lives*

Human blunders usually do more to shape history than human wickedness.

— A. J. P. TAYLOR (1906–1990), *The Origins of the Second World War,* 1960

The nature of peoples is first crude, then severe, then benign, then delicate, finally dissolute.

— GIAMBATTISTA VICO (1688–1744), *The New Science,* 1744

It is not love that should be depicted as blind, but self-love.

— VOLTAIRE (1694–1778), letter, May 11, 1764

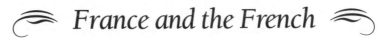

France and the French

France was long a despotism tempered by epigrams.

— THOMAS CARLYLE (1795–1881), *History of the French Revolution,* 1837

England is an empire; Germany is a nation, a race; France is a person.

— JULES MICHELET (1798–1874), *History of France,* 1867

The moment Germany rises as a great power, France gains a new importance as a *cultural power.*

— FRIEDRICH NIETZSCHE (1844–1900), *Twilight of the Idols,* 1889

Gentlemen

There were gentlemen and there were seamen in the navy of Charles the Second. But the seamen were not gentlemen; and the gentlemen were not seamen.

━ THOMAS BABINGTON MACAULAY (1800–1859), *History of England,* 1849

Germany and the Germans

[On the German language:] A frightful dialect for the stupid, the pedant and dullard sort.

━ THOMAS CARLYLE (1795–1881), *History of Frederick II,* 1858–1865

Everything ponderous, viscous, and pompously clumsy, all long-winded and wearying species of style are developed in profuse variety among Germans.

━ FRIEDRICH NIETZSCHE (1844–1900), *Beyond Good and Evil,* 1886

How much dreary heaviness, lameness, dampness, sloppiness, how much *beer* there is in the German intellect!

━ FRIEDRICH NIETZSCHE (1844–1900), *Twilight of the Idols,* 1889

Germany has reduced savagery to a science, and this great war for the victorious peace of justice must go on until the German cancer is cut clean out of the world body.

━ THEODORE ROOSEVELT (1858–1919), speech, September 30, 1917

The Germans—once they were called the nation of thinkers: do they still think at all? Nowadays the Germans are bored with intellect, the Germans mistrust intellect, politics devours all seriousness for really intellectual things—*Deutschland, Deutschland über alles* was, I fear, the end of German philosophy.

— FRIEDRICH NIETZSCHE (1844–1900), *Twilight of the Idols,* 1889

When they are not at war, they do a little hunting, but spend most of their time in idleness, sleeping and eating. The strongest and most warlike do nothing. They vegetate, while the care of hearth and home and fields is left to the women, the old and the weak. Strange inconsistency of temperament, which makes the same men lovers of sloth and haters of tranquility.

— TACITUS (ca. 55–ca. 120), *Germania*

God and Religion

Then I was standing on the highest mountain of them all. . . . And I saw that the sacred hoop of my people was one of many hoops that made one circle, wide as daylight and as starlight, and in the center grew one mighty flowering tree to shelter all the children of one mother and one father. And I saw that it was holy.

— BLACK ELK (1862–1950), in John G. Neihardt, *Black Elk Speaks,* 1961

It is accepted as an axiom by all Americans that the civil power ought to be not only neutral and impartial as between different forms of faith, but ought to leave these matters entirely on one side, regarding them no more than it regards the artistic or literary pursuits of the citizens.

— JAMES BRYCE (1838–1922), *The American Commonwealth,* 1888

What preoccupies us, then, is not God as a fact of nature, but as a fabrication useful for a God-fearing society. God himself becomes not a power but an image.

— DANIEL J. BOORSTIN (1914–   ), *The Image: A Guide to Pseudo-Events in America,* 1962

God is the Celebrity-Author of the World's Best Seller. We have made God into the biggest celebrity of all, to contain our own emptiness.

— DANIEL J. BOORSTIN (1914–   ), *The Image: A Guide to Pseudo-Events in America,* 1962

Like most lads among my boyhood associates, I learned the Ten Commandments. I was taught to reverence them because I was assured that they came down from the skies into hands of Moses, and that obedience to them was therefore sacredly incumbent upon me. I remember that whenever I fibbed, I found consolation in the fact that there was no commandment "Thou shalt not lie," and that the Decalogue forbade lying only as a "false witness" giving testimony before the courts where it might damage one's neighbor. In later years when I was much older, I began to be troubled by the fact that a code of morals which did not forbid lying seemed imperfect; but it was a long time before I raised the interesting question: How has my own realization of this imperfection arisen? Where did I myself get the moral yardstick by which I discovered this shortcoming in the Decalogue?

— JAMES HENRY BREASTED (1865–1935), *The Dawn of Conscience,* 1933

It is important to bear in mind the now commonly accepted fact that in its primitive stages, religion had nothing to do with morals as understood by us today.

— JAMES HENRY BREASTED (1865–1935), *The Dawn of Conscience,* 1933

Worship is transcendent wonder.

— THOMAS CARLYLE (1795–1881), *On Heroes and Hero-Worship, and the Heroic in History,* 1841

If triangles made a god, they would give him three sides.

— CHARLES DE MONTESQUIEU (1689–1755), *Lettres persanes,* 1721

Of all the differences between the old world and the new, this is perhaps the most salient. Half the wars of Europe, half the internal troubles that have vexed European states . . . have arisen from theological differences or from the rival claims of Church and State. This whole vast chapter of debate and strife has remained virtually unopened in the United States. There is no Established Church. All religious bodies are equal before the law, and unrecognized by the law, except as voluntary associations of private citizens.

— JAMES BRYCE (1838–1922), *The American Commonwealth,* 1888

The real security of Christianity is to be found in its benevolent morality, in its exquisite adaptation to the human heart, in the facility with which its scheme accommodates itself to the capacity of every human intellect, in the consolation which it bears to the house of mourning, in the light with which it brightens the great mystery of the grave.

— THOMAS BABINGTON MACAULAY (1800–1859), "Southey's Colloquies," 1830, reprinted in *Critical and Historical Essays,* 1843

Devout believers are safeguarded in a high degree against the risk of certain neurotic illnesses; their acceptance of the universal neurosis spares them the task of constructing a personal one.

— SIGMUND FREUD (1856–1939), *The Future of an Illusion,* 1927

Our knowledge of the historical worth of certain religious doctrines increases our respect for them, but does not invalidate our proposal that they should cease to be put forward as the reasons for the precepts of civilization. On the contrary! Those historical residues have helped us to view religious teachings, as it were, as neurotic relics, and we may now argue that the time has probably come, as it does in an analytic treatment, for replacing the effects of repression by the results of the rational operation of the intellect.

— SIGMUND FREUD (1856–1939), *The Future of an Illusion,* 1927

So much of truth, only under an ancient obsolete vesture, but the spirit of it still true, do I find in the paganism of old nations. Nature is still divine, the revelation of the workings of God; the Hero is still worshipable: this, under poor cramped incipient forms, is what all pagan religions have struggled, as they could, to set forth.

— THOMAS CARLYLE (1795–1881), *On Heroes and Hero-Worship, and the Heroic in History,* 1841

[Religious belief is] the universal obsessional neurosis of humanity.

— SIGMUND FREUD (1856–1939), *The Future of an Illusion,* 1927

All religions have based morality on obedience, that is to say, on voluntary slavery. That is why they have always been more pernicious than any political organisation. For the latter makes use of violence, the former—of the corruption of the will.

— ALEXANDER HERZEN (1812–1870), *From the Other Shore,* 1855

The Puritan hated bearbaiting, not because it gave pain to the bear, but because it gave pleasure to the spectators.

— THOMAS BABINGTON MACAULAY (1800–1859), *History of England,* 1849

A church is disaffected when it is persecuted, quiet when it is tolerated, and actively loyal when it is favoured and cherished.

— THOMAS BABINGTON MACAULAY (1800–1859), "Hallam," 1828, reprinted in *Critical and Historical Essays,* 1843

Religion is the sigh of the oppressed creature, the heart of a heartless world, and the soul of soulless conditions. It is the *opium* of the people.

— KARL MARX (1818–1883), *A Contribution to the Critique of Hegel's Philosophy of Right,* 1844

Life is a battle between faith and reason in which each feeds upon the other, drawing sustenance from it and destroying it.

— REINHOLD NIEBUHR (1892–1971), *Leaves from the Notebook of a Tamed Cynic,* 1930

A wise architect observed that you could break the laws of architectural art provided you had mastered them first. That would apply to religion as well as to art. Ignorance of the past does not guarantee freedom from its imperfections.

— REINHOLD NIEBUHR (1892–1971), *Leaves from the Notebook of a Tamed Cynic,* 1930

Two great European narcotics, alcohol and Christianity.

— FRIEDRICH NIETZSCHE (1844–1900), *Twilight of the Idols,* 1889

Wherever there are walls I shall inscribe this eternal accusation against Christianity upon them . . . I call Christianity the one great curse, the one great intrinsic depravity, the one great instinct for revenge for which no expedient is sufficiently poisonous, secret, subterranean, petty—I call it the one immortal blemish of mankind . . .

— FRIEDRICH NIETZSCHE (1844–1900), *The Anti-Christ,* 1895

There is in general good reason to suppose that in several respects the gods could all benefit from instruction by us human beings. We humans are—more humane.

— FRIEDRICH NIETZSCHE (1844–1900), *Beyond Good and Evil,* 1886

Despotism may govern without faith, but liberty cannot. . . . How is it possible that society should escape destruction if the moral tie is not strengthened in proportion as the political tie is relaxed? And what can be done with a people who are their own masters if they are not submissive to the Deity?

— ALEXIS DE TOCQUEVILLE (1805–1859), *Democracy in America,* 1840

Though it is very important for man as an individual that his religion should be true, that is not the case for society. Society has nothing to fear or hope from another life; what is most important for it is not that all citizens profess the true religion but that they should profess religion.

— ALEXIS DE TOCQUEVILLE (1805–1859), *Democracy in America,* 1840

I fear we are not getting rid of God because we still believe in grammar.

— FRIEDRICH NIETZSCHE (1844–1900), *Twilight of the Idols*, 1889

When an opinion has taken root in a democracy and established itself in the minds of the majority, it afterward persists by itself, needing no effort to maintain it since no one attacks it. Those who at first rejected it as false come in the end to adopt it as accepted, and even those who still at the bottom of their hearts oppose it keep their views to themselves, taking great care to avoid a dangerous and futile contest.

— ALEXIS DE TOCQUEVILLE (1805–1859), *Democracy in America*, 1840

The main business of religions is to purify, control, and restrain that excessive and exclusive taste for well-being which men acquire in times of equality.

— ALEXIS DE TOCQUEVILLE (1805–1859), *Democracy in America*, 1840

The brotherhood of Man presupposes the fatherhood of God.

— A. J. TOYNBEE (1889–1975), *A Study of History*, 1939

God is not on the side of the big battalions, but on the side of those who shoot best.

— VOLTAIRE (1694–1778), *Notebooks*, published 1968

If there were only one religion in England, there would be danger of despotism, if there were two, they would cut each other's throats, but there are 30, and they live in peace and happiness.

— VOLTAIRE (1694–1778), *Letters on England*, 1732

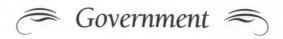

Government

The best reason why Monarchy is a strong government is that it is an intelligible government. The mass of mankind understand it, and they hardly anywhere in the world understand any other.

— WALTER BAGEHOT (1826–1877), *The English Constitution,* 1867

In the long run every Government is the exact symbol of its People, with their wisdom and unwisdom; we have to say, Like People like Government.

— THOMAS CARLYLE (1795–1881), *Past and Present,* 1843

Men are to be guided only by their self-interests. Good government is a good balancing of these; and, except a keen eye and appetite for self-interest, requires no virtue in any quarter. To both parties it is emphatically a machine: to the discontented, a "taxing-machine"; to the contented, a "machine for securing property." Its duties and its faults are not those of a father, but of an active parish-constable.

— THOMAS CARLYLE (1795–1881), *Signs of the Times,* 1829

Lives the man that can figure a naked Duke of Windlestraw addressing a naked House of Lords?

— THOMAS CARLYLE (1795–1881), *Sartor Resartus,* 1836

The Few assume to be the *deputies,* but they are often only the *despoilers* of the Many.

— GEORG HEGEL (1770–1831), *The Philosophy of History,* 1837

Nothing is so galling to a people not broken in from the birth as a paternal, or in other words a meddling government, a government which tells them what to read and say and eat and drink and wear.

— THOMAS BABINGTON MACAULAY (1800–1859), "Southey's *Colloquies on Society,*" 1830, reprinted in *Critical and Historical Essays,* 1843

Civil servants and priests, soldiers and ballet dancers, schoolmasters and police constables, Greek museums and Gothic steeples, civil list and services list—the common seed within which all these fabulous beings slumber in embryo is taxation.

— KARL MARX (1818–1883), *Moralizing Criticism and Critical Morality,* 1847

The anarchist and the Christian have a common origin.

— FRIEDRICH NIETZSCHE (1844–1900), *The Anti-Christ,* 1895

The Athenians govern the Greeks; I govern the Athenians; you, my wife, govern me; your son governs you.

— PLUTARCH (before 50–after 120), quoting Themistocles (ca. 528–ca. 462 B.C.), *Parallel Lives*

There is something to be said for government by a great aristocracy which has furnished leaders to the nation in peace and war for generations; even a democrat like myself must admit this. But there is absolutely nothing to be said for government by a plutocracy, for government by men very powerful in certain lines and gifted with the "money touch," but with ideals which in their essence are merely those of so many glorified pawnbrokers.

— THEODORE ROOSEVELT (1858–1919), letter, November 15, 1913

Grant me 30 years of equal division of inheritances and a free press, and I will provide you with a republic.

— ALEXIS DE TOCQUEVILLE (1805–1859), *Democracy in America,* 1840

Governments need to have both shepherds and butchers.

— VOLTAIRE (1694–1778), *Notebooks,* published 1968

In general, the art of government consists in taking as much money as possible from one party of the citizens to give to the other.

— VOLTAIRE (1694–1778), entry on "Money" in *Philosophical Dictionary,* 1764

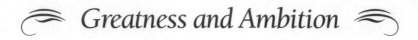 *Greatness and Ambition*

No great man lives in vain. The history of the world is but the biography of great men.

— THOMAS CARLYLE (1795–1881), *On Heroes, Hero-Worship, and the Heroic in History,* 1841

The world cannot live at the level of its great men.

— SIR JAMES GEORGE FRAZER (1854–1941), *The Golden Bough,* 1922

The desire for glory clings even to the best men longer than any other passion.

— TACITUS (ca. 56–ca. 120), *Histories*

In my opinion, most of the great men of the past were only there for the beer—the wealth, prestige and grandeur that went with the power.

— A. J. P. TAYLOR (1906–1990), quoted in Peter Vansittart, *Voices 1870–1914,* 1984

 *Greed*

Avarice, the spur of industry.

— DAVID HUME (1711–1776), "Of Civil Liberty," in *Essays Moral, Political, and Literary,* 1742

Men hate the individual whom they call avaricious only because nothing can be gained from him.

— VOLTAIRE (1694–1778), entry on "Avarice" in *Philosophical Dictionary,* 1764

The wish to acquire more is admittedly a very natural and common thing; and when men succeed in this they are always praised rather than condemned. But when they lack the ability to do so and yet want to acquire more at all costs, they deserve condemnation for their mistakes.

➤ NICCOLÒ MACHIAVELLI (1469–1527), *The Prince*, 1514

Happiness

But the whim we have of happiness is somewhat thus. By certain valuations, and averages, of our own striking, we come upon some sort of average terrestrial lot; this we fancy belongs to us by nature, and of indefeasible rights. It is simple payment of our wages, of our deserts; requires neither thanks nor complaint. . . . Foolish soul! What act of legislature was there that *thou* shouldst be happy? A little while ago thou hadst no right to be at all.

➤ THOMAS CARLYLE (1795–1881), *Sartor Resartus*, 1836

[Happiness is] the (preferably sudden) satisfaction of needs which have been dammed up to a high degree.

➤ SIGMUND FREUD (1856–1939), *Civilization and Its Discontents*, 1930

One feels inclined to say that the intention that man should be "happy" is not included in the plan of "Creation."

➤ SIGMUND FREUD (1856–1939), *Civilization and Its Discontents*, 1930

The history of the world is not the theatre of happiness. Periods of happiness are blank pages in it, for they are periods of harmony— periods when the antithesis is in abeyance.

➤ GEORG HEGEL (1770–1831), *The Philosophy of History*, 1837

No man who has once heartily and wholly laughed can be altogether irreclaimably bad.

— THOMAS CARLYLE (1795–1881), *Sartor Resartus,* 1836

The great end of all human industry is the attainment of happiness. For this were arts invented, sciences cultivated, laws ordained, and societies modelled, by the most profound wisdom of patriots and legislators. Even the lonely savage, who lies exposed to the inclemency of the elements and the fury of wild beasts, forgets not, for a moment, this grand object of his being.

— DAVID HUME (1711–1776), "The Stoic," in *Essays Moral, Political, and Literary,* 1742

 *Heroism*

Celebrity-worship and hero-worship should not be confused. Yet we confuse them every day, and by doing so we come dangerously close to depriving ourselves of all real models. We lose sight of the men and women who do not simply seem great because they are famous but are famous because they are great. We come closer and closer to degrading all fame into notoriety.

— DANIEL J. BOORSTIN (1914–   ), *The Image: A Guide to Pseudo-Events in America,* 1961

In our world of big names, curiously, our true heroes tend to be anonymous. In this life of illusion and quasi-illusion, the person of solid virtues who can be admired for something more substantial than his well-knownness often proves to be the unsung hero: the teacher, the nurse, the mother, the honest cop, the hard worker at lonely, underpaid, unglamorous, unpublicized jobs.

— DANIEL J. BOORSTIN (1914–   ), *The Image: A Guide to Pseudo-Events in America,* 1961

No sadder proof can be given by a man of his own littleness than disbelief in great men.

— THOMAS CARLYLE (1795–1881), *On Heroes, Hero-Worship, and the Heroic in History,* 1841

Once the state has been founded, there can no longer be any heroes. They come on the scene only in uncivilized conditions.

— GEORG HEGEL (1770–1831), *The Philosophy of Right,* 1821

The hero in history is the individual to whom we can justifiably attribute preponderant influence in determining an issue or event whose consequences would have been profoundly different if he had not acted as he did.

— SIDNEY HOOK (1902–1989), *The Hero in History: A Study in Limitation and Possibility,* 1943

[The hero] finds a fork in the historical road, but he also helps, so to speak, to create it. He increases the odds of success for the alternative he chooses by virtue of the extraordinary qualities he brings to bear to realize it.

— SIDNEY HOOK (1902–1989), *The Hero in History: A Study in Limitation and Possibility,* 1943

Heroes are created by popular demand, sometimes out of the scantiest materials, or none at all.

— GERALD WHITE JOHNSON (1890–1980), *American Heroes and Hero-Worship,* 1943

Heroes are such because of monomaniacal determination. They are rarely pleasant men; their rigidity approaches the fanatic.

— HENRY A. KISSINGER (1923–   ), *White House Years,* 1979

And how can man die better
Than facing fearful odds,
For the ashes of his fathers,
And the temples of his Gods?

— THOMAS BABINGTON MACAULAY (1800–1859), "Horatius," in *Lays of Ancient Rome,* 1842

Historians
and the Historian's Craft

Advice to persons about to write history—don't.
— LORD ACTON (1834–1902), letter, April 5, 1887

Historical understanding consists of perceiving difference among similar phenomena *and* similarities among different ones.
— RAYMOND ARON, "Evidence and Inference in History," in Daniel Lerner, ed., *Evidence and Inference,* 1959

It is the true office of history to represent the events themselves, together with the counsels, and to leave the observations and conclusions thereupon to the liberty and faculty of every man's judgment.
— FRANCIS BACON (1561–1626), *Advancement of Learning,* 1605

As a historian, I am perfectly prepared to do without "inevitable," "unavoidable," "inescapable," and even "ineluctable." Life will be drabber. But let us leave them to poets and metaphysicians.
— E. H. CARR (1892–1982), *What Is History?* 1962

Historian. A broad-gauge gossip.
— AMBROSE BIERCE (1842–1914), *The Devil's Dictionary,* 1881–1906

If the historian has any function in the present welter of the social scientific world, it is to note the rich particularity of experience, to search for the piquant aroma of life. As contrasted with the abstract, antiseptic dullness of numbers, "cases," and prototypes. The historian as humanist is a votary of the unrepeatability of all experience, as well as of the universal significance of human life.
— DANIEL J. BOORSTIN (1914–   ), *America and the Image of Europe,* 1960

Writers, like teeth, are divided into incisors and grinders.
— WALTER BAGEHOT (1826–1877), *Estimates of Some Englishmen and Scotchmen,* 1858

History has a history.
— KELLY BOYD, Introduction to *Encyclopedia of Historians and Historical Writing,* 1999

Academic historians remain committed to their discipline even if they differ about what that discipline exactly is. They revel in the complexity and the opportunity to seek out new areas for study. They persist in stressing that people in the past experienced material realities from day to day, and they valorize rigorous attempts to uncover the past and try to understand it. They use theory to help them understand the possibilities of interpretation rather than to substitute for the necessarily painstaking research required of them. They struggle to write for the general reader. Historical writing remains dynamic at the start of the third millennium.
— KELLY BOYD, Introduction to *Encyclopedia of Historians and Historical Writing,* 1999

What the metahistorian and the sociologist are trying to do is to clear away the confusion of facts and reveal the pattern, or establish the law, which lies beneath. But this is not the historian's purpose; what he wants to know is what happened. For him, general propositions are both necessary and illuminating, but they are not the essential purpose of his work.
— ALLAN BULLOCK (1914–), "The Historian's Purpose: History and Metahistory," *History Today,* February 1951

[Of Edward Gibbon:]
And hiving wisdom with each studious year,
In meditation dwelt, with learning wrought,
And shaped his weapon with an edge severe,
Sapping a solemn creed with solemn sneer.
— LORD BYRON (1788–1824), *Childe Harold's Pilgrimage,* 1818

It is no doubt important to know that the great battle was fought in 1066 and not in 1065 or 1067, and that it was fought at Hastings and not Eastbourne or Brighton. The historian must not get these things wrong. But when points of this kind are raised, I am reminded of Houseman's remarks that "accuracy is a duty, not a virtue." To praise a historian for his accuracy is like praising an architect for using well-seasoned timber or properly mixed concrete in the building. It is a necessary condition of his work, but not his essential function.

— E. H. CARR (1892–1982), *What Is History?* 1962

The main work of the historian is not to record, but to evaluate; for, if he does not evaluate, how can he know what is worth recording?

— E. H. CARR (1892–1982), *What Is History?* 1961

The historian, by the very nature of his task, must be concerned with change. What made for change? Why did it come when it did, and in the way it did? These are characteristically historians' questions.

— ALFRED D. CHANDLER, JR. (1918–   ), *Business History Review* (spring 1959)

Writing a book is an adventure. To begin with, it is a toy and an amusement; then it becomes a mistress, and then it becomes a master, and then a tyrant.

— WINSTON CHURCHILL (1874–1965), quoted in William Safire, "Gifts of Gab for '95," *New York Times Magazine* (December 18, 1994)

Preconceived notions are a much greater danger to historical truth than either deficiency of evidence or error in detail. . . . The historian must certainly make one initial choice, of main area of study or line of approach. But after that (if he is worth considering at all) he becomes the servant of his evidence of which he will, or should, ask no specific questions until he has absorbed what it says.

— G. R. ELTON (1921–1994), *The Practice of History,* 1967

A moment's reflection should suffice to establish the simple proposition that every historian, willy-nilly, must begin his research with a question. Questions are the engines of intellect, the cerebral machines which convert energy into to motion, and curiosity to controlled inquiry. There can be no thinking without questioning no purposeful study of the past, nor any serious planning for the future.

⟶ DAVID HACKETT FISCHER (1935–   ), *Historians' Fallacies: Toward a Logic of Historical Thought,* 1970

The historical imagination . . . is properly not ornamental but structural. Without it the historian would have no narrative to adorn. The imagination, that "blind but indispensable faculty" without which, as Kant has shown, we could never perceive the world around us, is indispensable in the same way to history.

⟶ R. G. COLLINGWOOD, *The Idea of History,* 1946

Scissors-and-paste historians study periods; they collect all the extant testimony about a certain limited group of events, and hope in vain that something will come of it. Scientific historians study problems: they ask questions, and if they are good historians they ask questions which they see their way to answering.

⟶ R. G. COLLINGWOOD (1889–1943), quoted in David Hackett Fischer, *Historians' Fallacies: Toward a Logic of Historical Thought,* 1970

The historian's job is to aggrandize, promoting accident to inevitability and innocuous circumstance to portent.

⟶ PETER CONRAD (1948–   ), *The Art of the City,* 1984

What distinguishes the historian from the collector of historical facts is generalization.

⟶ G. R. ELTON (1921–1994), *The Practice of History,* 1967

History repeats itself. Historians repeat each other.

⟶ PHILIP GUEDALLA (1889–1944), *Supers and Supermen,* 1920

A historian, like any other researcher, has a vested interest in answering his own questions. His job is at stake, and his reputation, and most important, his self-respect.

— DAVID HACKETT FISCHER (1935–   ), *Historians' Fallacies: Toward a Logic of Historical Thought*, 1970

At the Boston Athenaeum, one may discover flocks of tiny birdlike old gentlemen, who nest in eery piles of dirty yellow paper and brood their myths and memories into monumental Lives-and-Letters. In every New England town library, there is likely to be an ancient Puritan virgin, shriveled and dried in the snows of 60 Massachusetts winters and suitably shrouded in black bombazine, who has been at work for the past 20 years on the story of her hometown from 1633 to 1933, when Franklin Roosevelt was inaugurated and history came to an end.

— DAVID HACKETT FISCHER (1935–   ), *Historians' Fallacies: Toward a Logic of Historical Thought*, 1970

I can see . . . only one safe rule for the historian: that he should recognize in the development of human destinies the play of the contingent and the unforeseen.

— H. A. L. FISHER (1865–1940), *History of Europe*, 1935

The historian must have . . . some conception of how men who are not historians behave. Otherwise he will move in a world of the dead. He can only gain that conception through personal experience, and he can only use his personal experiences when he is a genius.

— E. M. FORSTER (1879–1970), "Captain Edward Gibbon," 1931, in *Abinger Harvest*, 1936

You treat world history as a mathematician does mathematics, in which nothing but laws and formulas exist, no reality, no good and evil, no time, no yesterday, no tomorrow, nothing but an eternal, shallow, mathematical present.

— HERMANN HESSE (1877–1962), *The Glass Bead Game*, 1943

One cannot be a good historian of the outward, visible world without giving some thought to the hidden, private life of ordinary people; and on the other hand one cannot be a good historian of this inner life without taking into account outward events where these are relevant. They are two orders of fact which reflect each other, which are always linked and which sometimes provoke each other.

— VICTOR HUGO (1802–1885), *Les Misérables*, 1862

Great abilities are not requisite for an Historian; for in historical composition, all the greatest powers of the human mind are quiescent. He has facts ready to his hand; so there is no exercise of invention. Imagination is not required in any degree; only about as much as is used in the lowest kinds of poetry. Some penetration, accuracy, and colouring will fit a man for the task, if he can give the application which is necessary.

— SAMUEL JOHNSON (1709–1784), spoken in 1763, quoted in James Boswell, *Life of Samuel Johnson*, 1791

A good many historical arguments are objectionable not because they are fallacious, but because they are banal, shallow, or trivial. As a remedy for these failings, logic is impotent.

— DAVID HACKETT FISCHER (1935–   ), *Historians' Fallacies: Toward a Logic of Historical Thought*, 1970

I love those historians that are either very simple or most excellent. . . . Such as are between both (which is the most common fashion), it is they that spoil all; they will needs chew our meat for us and take upon them a law to judge, and by consequence to square and incline the story according to their fantasy.

— MICHEL DE MONTAIGNE (1533–1592), "Of Books," in *Essays*, 1580

Historians begin by looking backward. They often end by thinking backward.

— FRIEDRICH NIETZSCHE (1844–1900), quoted in David Hackett Fischer, *Historians' Fallacies: Toward a Logic of Historical Thought*, 1970

Historian—An unsuccessful novelist.

— H. L. MENCKEN (1880–1956), "Sententiæ: The Mind of Men," in *A Mencken Chrestomathy*, 1949

Somebody once asked Thomas Edison about his rules of procedure and received a rude reply: "Rules!" Said Edison. "Hell! There ain't no rules around here! We're tryin' to accomplish sump'n." A good many historians, particularly of the present permissive generation, which has made a cult of flexibility in its procedures, seem to have formed the same idea of their own discipline.

— DAVID HACKETT FISCHER (1935–   ), *Historians' Fallacies: Toward a Logic of Historical Thought*, 1970

Logical and methodological techniques are not ends but means. It would be unfortunate if historians were to become so obsessed by problems of how to do their work that no work could ever get done.

— DAVID HACKETT FISCHER (1935–   ), *Historians' Fallacies: Toward a Logic of Historical Thought*, 1970

A historian must not merely get the facts right. He must get the right facts right.

— DAVID HACKETT FISCHER (1935–   ), *Historians' Fallacies: Toward a Logic of Historical Thought*, 1970

. . . an historian must not merely provide good relevant evidence but the best relevant evidence. And the best relevant evidence, all things being equal, is evidence which is most nearly immediate to the event itself.

— DAVID HACKETT FISCHER (1935–   ), *Historians' Fallacies: Toward a Logic of Historical Thought*, 1970

One of my greatest pleasures in writing has come from the thought that perhaps my work might annoy someone of comfortably pretentious position. Then comes the saddening realization that such people rarely read.

— JOHN KENNETH GALBRAITH (1908–   ), *A Life in Our Times: Memoirs*, 1981

To write history, or even to read it, is to be endlessly engaged in a process of selection. No part of the job is more difficult or more important, and yet no part has been studied with less system, or practiced with less method. Many facts are called, but few are consciously chosen, on explicit and rational criteria of factual significance.

— DAVID HACKETT FISCHER (1935–   ), *Historians' Fallacies: Toward a Logic of Historical Thought,* 1970

Scholars solemnly engage in controversies over questions such as "Should a historian generalize?" One might as well ask "Should a historian use words?" Generalizations are embedded in his language, in his thought, and in his explanation models. There are, of course, other modes of explanation. But none is more common, or more commonly abused, than generalization.

— DAVID HACKETT FISCHER (1935–   ), *Historians' Fallacies: Toward a Logic of Historical Thought,* 1970

As historians we are committed to the idea that history is an art as well as a science but that making history interesting to nonspecialists does not require either simplifying or embellishing past events.

— ERIC FONER and JOHN A. GARRATY, *The Reader's Companion to American History,* 1991

Since [the historian] cannot know the cause beforehand, he should not be content to study a specific category of facts; he should carefully observe all the facts, all the institutions, all regulations public and private, all the customs of domestic life, and particularly everything that relates to the possession of land. He should study all of these things with equally careful attention, for he does not know beforehand from which side enlightenment will come to him. This method is slow, but it is the only one which is sure.

— FUSTEL DE COULANGES, *Histoire des Institutions Politiques de l'Ancienne France,* 1890

To do history, one must know how to count.

— GEORGES LEFEBVRE (1874–1959), quoted in David Hackett Fischer, *Historians' Fallacies: Toward a Logic of Historical Thought,* 1970

We need to know how and why we use history to serve both our needs of personal and group identity as well as for the more "scientific" and humanistic purposes of historical analysis. We should know the differences and not confound them.

━ NATHAN IRVIN HUGGINS (1927–), 1983, quoted in Stanley I. Kutler, ed., *American Retrospectives: Historians on Historians*, 1995

I have *not* tried to write definitive history in any of my books, among other reasons because I think it impossible except for small subjects, tightly limited in purpose.

━ FRANCIS JENNINGS (1918–), *Empire of Fortune: Crowns, Colonies, and Tribes in the Seven Years War in America*, 1988

By pressing methodological norms too far we may inhibit bold and imaginative adventures of ideas. The irony is that methodology itself may make for conformism—conformity to its own favored reconstructions.

━ ABRAHAM KAPLAN (1918–), *The Conduct of Inquiry*, 1964

The perfect historian is he in whose work the character and spirit of an age is exhibited in miniature.

━ THOMAS BABBINGTON MACAULAY (1800–1859), "History," 1828, in *Critical and Historical Essays Contributed to the Edinburgh Review*, 1843

A big part of writing a book, a biography or history, is in what's called in too fancy a way, the analysis. You collect all of the materal. That's the research, and that's wonderful fun. That's joy. That's like working on a detective case. The hard stuff is the writing. And there's that point where you have to take all this material you've gathered and put it out on the table—and look at it and think about it. That's why the books take so long. You have to think so much about it. And writing is thinking. That's what makes it so hard. And to write well is really to think clearly.

━ DAVID MCCULLOUGH (1933–), interview with Roger Mudd, in *Great Minds of History*, 1999

[Narrative history] unfolds as the events unfolded in time, and you're inside the narrative, the story. You are not seeing it from the grand mountaintop, or the grand advantage of the present, looking out over the past and pontificating about it. You are in the event. You are inside that time. I want a reader to have the feeling of having lived in a distant, different, vanished time. And I want a reader to sense that those were real human beings, and that they didn't know how it was going to come out, anymore than we do in our time.

⏤ DAVID McCULLOUGH (1933–   ), interview with Roger Mudd,
in *Great Minds of History,* 1999

The hardest thing to convey in writing history or teaching history is that nothing ever had to happen the way it happened.

⏤ DAVID McCULLOUGH (1933–   ), interview with Roger Mudd,
in *Great Minds of History,* 1999

The challenge [in writing history] is to get the reader beyond thinking that things had to be the way they turned out and to see the range of possibilities of how it could have been otherwise.

⏤ DAVID McCULLOUGH (1933–   ), quoted in Esther B. Fein,
"Immersed in Facts, to Touch Truman's Life," *The New York Times,* August 14, 1992

I think most historians are interested in trying to explain causes, consequences, reasons. They're interested in "why" questions— Why did this happen?—and in some of the "what" questions— What are the consequences? But I am personally convinced that you can't really understand the why questions, the causal questions, unless you understand the actual events. And in fact, events themselves become causes.

⏤ JAMES McPHERSON (1943–   ), interview with Roger Mudd,
in *Great Minds of History,* 1999

A few hints as to literary craftsmanship may be useful to budding historians. First and foremost, *get writing!*

⏤ SAMUEL ELIOT MORISON (1887–1976), *History as a Literary Art,* 1946

The function of the historian is akin to that of the painter and not of the photographic camera: to discover and set forth, to single out and stress that which is of the nature of the thing, and not to reproduce indiscriminately all that meets the eye.

— SIR LEWIS NAMIER (1888–1960), *Avenues of History,* 1952

It is evident that other study than that of the closet is indispensable to success in [writing about the American Indian]. Habits of early reading had greatly aided to prepare me for the task; but necessary knowledge of a more practical kind has been supplied by the indulgence of a strong natural taste, which, at various intervals, led me to the wild regions of the north and west. Here, by the campfire, or in the canoe, I gained familiar acquaintance with the men and scenery of the wilderness.

— FRANCIS PARKMAN (1823–1893), *The Conspiracy of Pontiac,* 1870

Historians desiring to write the actions of men, ought to set down the simple truth, and not say anything for love or hatred; also to choose such an opportunity for writing as it may be lawful to think what they will, and write what they think, which is a rare happiness of the time.

— SIR WALTER RALEIGH (1552–1618), *The Cabinet Council,* published 1751

Historians are left forever chasing shadows, painfully aware of their inability ever to reconstruct a dead world in its completeness however thorough or revealing their documentation. . . . We are doomed to be forever hailing someone who has just gone around the corner and out of earshot.

— SIMON SCHAMA (1945–   ), *Dead Certainties,* 1991

History, taught for a directly and immediately useful purpose to pupils and the teachers of pupils, is one of the necessary features of a sound education in democratic citizenship.

— THEODORE ROOSEVELT (1858–1919), *History and Literature and Other Essays,* 1913

The true historian will bring the past before our eyes as if it were present. He will make us see as living men the hard-faced archers of Agincourt, and the war-worn spearmen who followed Alexander down beyond the rim of the known world. . . . We shall also see the supreme righteousness of the wars for freedom and justice, and know that the men who fell in those wars made all mankind their debtors.

— THEODORE ROOSEVELT (1858–1919), speech to the American Historical Association, December 17, 1912

The vision of the great historian must be both wide and lofty.

— THEODORE ROOSEVELT (1858–1919), *History and Literature and Other Essays*, 1913

The great speeches of statesmen and the great writings of historians can live only if they possess the deathless quality that inheres in all great literature.

— THEODORE ROOSEVELT (1858–1919), *History and Literature and Other Essays*, 1913

Many learned people seem to feel that the quality of readableness in a book is one which warrants suspicion. Indeed, not a few learned people seem to feel that the fact that a book is interesting is proof that it is shallow.

— THEODORE ROOSEVELT (1858–1919), *History and Literature and Other Essays*, 1913

Ignorance is the first requisite of the historian—ignorance, which simplifies and clarifies, which selects and omits, with a placid perfection unattainable by the highest art.

— LYTTON STRACHEY (1880–1932), *Eminent Victorians*, 1918

What his imagination is to the poet, facts are to the historian. His exercise of judgment comes in their selection, his art in their arrangement.

— BARBARA TUCHMAN (1912–1989), book review, *The New York Times*, 1964

The historian is a prophet looking backwards.

— FRIEDRICH VON SCHLEGEL (1772–1829), *Dialogue on Poetry and Literary Aphorisms*, 1800

The historian must recognize that history is not a scientific enterprise but a moral one.

— PAGE SMITH (1917–1995), *The Historian and History*, 1964

The continual rearrangement of the past to suit current prejudices is . . . the historian's work.

— RONALD STEEL (1931–   ), *New York Review of Books*, September 24, 1981

Thucydides, an Athenian, wrote the history of the war between the Peloponnesians and the Athenians; he began at the moment that it broke out, believing that it would be a great war, and more memorable than any that had preceded it.

— THUCYDIDES (ca. 460–400 B.C.), *The History of the Peloponnesian War*, 431–413 B.C.

With reference to the narrative of events, far from permitting myself to derive it from the first source that came to hand, I did not even trust my own impressions, but it rests partly on what I saw myself, partly on what others saw for me, the accuracy of the report being always tried by the most severe and detailed tests possible.

— THUCYDIDES (ca. 460–400 B.C.), *The History of the Peloponnesian War*, 431–413 B.C.

Study men, not historians.

— HARRY S. TRUMAN (1884–1972), quoted in Robert H. Ferrell, *Off the Record*, 1980

It seems to me if you're trapped in storytelling, it's not necessarily such a bad trap. That's just the way that we understand the world, and we should tell the best, most compelling stories we can.

— RICHARD WHITE (1947–   ), interview with Roger Mudd, in *Great Minds of History*, 1999

To be a best-seller is not necessarily a measure of quality, but it is a measure of communication.
 ➤ BARBARA TUCHMAN (1912–1989), speech, 1966

Anybody can make history. Only a great man can write it.
 ➤ OSCAR WILDE (1854–1900), *The Critic as Artist*, 1891

To give an accurate description of what has never occurred is not merely the proper occupation of the historian, but the inalienable privilege of any man of parts and culture.
 ➤ OSCAR WILDE (1854–1900), *The Critic as Artist*, 1891

The meaning . . . of a writer will be found not just in what he intends to say, or what he does literally say, but in the effect of his writing on living beings.
 ➤ HOWARD ZINN (1922–   ), *The Politics of History*, 1970

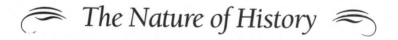

The Nature of History

History is a relay of revolutions.
 ➤ SAUL ALINSKY (1909–1972), "Of Means and Ends," *Rules for Radicals,* 1971

History is, strictly speaking, the study of questions; the study of answers belongs to anthropology and sociology.
 ➤ W. H. AUDEN (1907–1973), *The Dyer's Hand,* 1962

A year that ends in a "0" is bound to seem significant; one that ends in "00," even more significant; and one that ends in "000," most significant of all.
 ➤ ISAAC ASIMOV (1920–1992), *Asimov's Chronology of the World,* 1991

History, real solemn history, I cannot be interested in. . . . I read it a little as a duty; but it tells me nothing that does not either vex or weary me. The quarrels of popes and kings, with wars and pestilences in every page; the men all so good for nothing, and hardly any women at all.
—JANE AUSTEN (1775–1817), *Northanger Abbey,* 1818

Histories make men wise; poets witty; the mathematics subtle; natural philosophy deep; morals grave; logic and rhetoric able to contend.
—FRANCIS BACON (1561–1626), "Of Studies," in *Essays,* 1625

The best history is but like the art of Rembrandt; it casts a vivid light on certain selected causes, on those which were best and greatest; it leaves all the rest in shadow and unseen.
—WALTER BAGEHOT (1826–1877), *Physics and Politics,* 1872

American history is longer, larger, more various, more beautiful, and more terrible than anything anyone has ever said about it.
—JAMES BALDWIN (1924–1987), "A Talk To Teachers," 1963, in *Collected Essays,* 1998

Any written history inevitably reflects the thought of the author in his time and cultural setting.
—CHARLES A. BEARD (1874–1948), "Written History as an Act of Faith," *American Historical Review,* January 1934

Only three broad conceptions of all history as actuality are possible. History is chaos and every attempt to interpret it otherwise is an illusion. History moves around in a kind of cycle. History moves in a line, straight or spiral, and in some direction. The historian may seek to escape these issues by silence or by a confession of avoidance or he may face them boldly, aware of the intellectual and moral perils inherent in any decision—in his act of faith.
—CHARLES A. BEARD (1874–1948), "Written History as an Act of Faith," *American Historical Review,* January 1934

Every time history repeats itself the price goes up.

⟵ ANONYMOUS

Civil history, particularly so called, is of prime dignity and authority among human writings; as the examples of antiquity, the revolutions of things, the foundations of civil prudence, with the names and reputations of men, are committed to its trust.

⟵ FRANCIS BACON (1561–1626), *The Advancement of Learning,* 1605

History. An account, mostly false, of events, mostly unimportant, which are brought about by rulers, mostly knaves, and soldiers, mostly fools.

⟵ AMBROSE BIERCE (1842–1914), *The Devil's Dictionary,* 1906

That great dust-heap called "history."

⟵ AUGUSTINE BIRRELL (1850–1933), "Carlyle," in *Obiter Dicta,* 1884

Acts themselves alone are history. . . . Tell me the acts, O historian, and leave me to reason upon them as I please; away with your reasoning and your rubbish! All that is not action is not worth reading.

⟵ WILLIAM BLAKE (1757–1827), *A Descriptive Catalogue,* 1809

Universal history is the history of a few metaphors.

⟵ JORGE LUIS BORGES (1899–1986), *Pascal's Sphere,* 1951

English history is all about men liking their fathers, and American history is all about men hating their fathers and trying to burn down everything they ever did.

⟵ MALCOLM BRADBURY (1932–   ), *Stepping Westward,* 1965

All true histories contain instruction; though, in some, the treasure may be hard to find, and when found, so trivial in quantity that the dry, shriveled kernel scarcely compensates for the trouble of cracking the nut.

⟵ ANNE BRONTË (1820–1849), *Agnes Grey,* 1847

Human history has been largely the story of migrations.
— HUGH BROGAN, *The Penguin History of the United States of America*, 1985

The chief practical use of history is to deliver us from plausible historical analogies.
— JAMES BRYCE (1838–1922), quoted in David Hackett Fischer, *Historians' Fallacies: Toward a Logic of Historical Thought*, 1970

History is the record of what one age finds worthy of note in another.
— JACOB BURCKHARDT (1818–1897), *Judgments on History and Historians*, 1929; translated 1958

The history of the world is the record of the weakness, frailty and death of public opinion.
— SAMUEL BUTLER (1835–1902), "Pictures and Books," in *Notebooks*, 1912

History, as an entirety, could only exist in the eyes of an observer outside it and outside the world. History only exists, in the final analysis, for God.
— ALBERT CAMUS (1913–1960), *The Rebel*, 1951

If man is reduced to being nothing but a character in history, he has no other choice but to subside into the sound and fury of a completely irrational history or to endow history with the form of human reason.
— ALBERT CAMUS (1913–1960), *The Rebel*, 1951

Happy the people whose annals are vacant.
— THOMAS CARLYLE (1795–1881), *History of the French Revolution*, 1837

History, a distillation of rumour.
— THOMAS CARLYLE (1795–1881), *History of the French Revolution*, 1837

The illimitable, silent, never-resting thing called Time, rolling, rushing on, swift, silent, like an all-embracing oceantide, on which we and all the universe swim like exhalations, like apparitions which *are,* and then *are not:* this is forever very literally a miracle; a thing to strike us dumb, for we have no word to speak about it.

> ← THOMAS CARLYLE (1795–1881), *On Heroes, Hero-Worship, and the Heroic in History,* 1841

What are your historical facts; still more your biographical? Wilt thou know a man . . . by stringing together beadrolls of what thou namest Facts?

> ← THOMAS CARLYLE (1795–1881), *Sartor Resartus,* 1834

Only the history of free peoples is worth our attention; the history of men under a despotism is merely a collection of anecdotes.

> ← SÉBASTIEN-ROCH NICOLAS DE CHAMFORT (1741–1794), *Maxims and Considerations,* 1796

History will bear me out, particularly as I shall write that history myself.

> ← WINSTON CHURCHILL (1874–1965), quoted in Timothy Garton Ash, "In the Churchill Museum," *New York Review of Books,* May 7, 1987

History is nothing but a procession of false Absolutes, a series of temples raised to pretexts, a degradation of the mind before the Improbable.

> ← E. M. CIORAN (1911–   ), *A Short History of Decay,* 1949

History is a vast early warning system.

> ← NORMAN COUSINS (1912–1990), "Editor's Odyssey: Gleanings from Articles and Editorials by N.C.," *Saturday Review,* April 15, 1978

[Regarding Voltaire:] He has invented history.

> ← MARQUISE DU DEFFAND (1697–1780), quoted in Fournier's *L'Esprit dans l'Historie,* 1857

The disadvantage of men not knowing the past is that they do not know the present. History is a hill or high point of vantage, from which alone men see the town in which they live or the age in which they are living.

    — G. K. CHESTERTON (1874–1936), "On St. George Revivified," in *All I Survey*, 1933

The bases for historical knowledge are not empirical facts but written texts, even if these texts masquerade in the guise of wars or revolutions.

    — PAUL DE MAN (1919–1983), "Literary History and Literary Modernity," 1969, reprinted in *Blindness and Insight*, 1971

History is the present. That's why every generation writes it anew. But what most people think of as history is its end product, myth.

    — E. L. DOCTOROW (1931–   ), in George Plimpton, ed., *Writers at Work*, 1988

We as women know that there are no disembodied processes; that all history originates in human flesh; that all oppression is inflicted by the body of one against the body of another; that all social change is built on the bone and muscle, and out of the flesh and blood, of human creators.

    — ANDREA DWORKIN (1946–   ), "Our Blood: The Slavery of Women in Amerika," 1975, published in *Our Blood*, 1976

A people without history
Is not redeemed from time, for history is a pattern
Of timeless moments.

    — T. S. ELIOT (1888–1965), "Little Gidding," in *Four Quartets*, 1943

No one reads or writes history in a fit of total absentmindedness, though a fair amount of history has been written by people whose minds seem in part to have been on other things.

    — G. R. ELTON (1921–1994), quoted in David Hackett Fischer, *Historians' Fallacies: Toward a Logic of Historical Thought*, 1970

[Written] history is largely the glorification of the iniquities of the triumphant.

— PAUL ELDRIDGE (1888–1982), *Maxims for a Modern Man*, 1965

Each generation does not rewrite the history books; it revises them.

— DAVID HACKETT FISCHER (1935–   ), *Historians' Fallacies: Toward a Logic of Historical Thought*, 1970

History is more or less bunk. It's tradition. We don't want tradition. We want to live in the present and the only history that is worth a tinker's damn is the history we make today.

— HENRY FORD (1863–1947), interview in *Chicago Tribune*, May 25, 1916

There is a sort of myth of History that philosophers have. . . . History for philosophers is some sort of great, vast continuity in which the freedom of individuals and economic or social determinations come and get entangled. When someone lays a finger on one of those great themes—continuity, the effective exercise of human liberty, how individual liberty is articulated with social determinations—when someone touches one of these three myths, these good people start crying out that History is being raped or murdered.

— MICHEL FOUCAULT (1926–1984), interview in *La Quinzaine Littéraire*, March 15, 1968

History . . . is, indeed, little more than the register of the crimes, follies, and misfortunes of mankind.

— EDWARD GIBBON (1737–1794), *The Decline and Fall of the Roman Empire*, 1776

There are only two great currents in the history of mankind: the baseness which makes conservatives and the envy which makes revolutionaries.

— EDMOND DE GONCOURT (1822–1896) and JULES DE GONCOURT (1830–1870), written 1867; published in *The Goncourt Journals*, 1888–1896

All our hopes for the future depend on a sound understanding of the past.

— FREDERIC HARRISON (1831–1923), written 1862, quoted in Alan Axelrod, *The Complete Idiot's Guide to 20th-Century History,* 1999

What experience and history teach is this—that people and governments never have learned anything from history, or acted on principles deduced from it.

— GEORG HEGEL (1770–1831), *Philosophy of History,* 1837

Regarding History as the slaughter-bench at which the happiness of peoples, the wisdom of States, and the virtue of individuals have been victimized—the question involuntarily arises—to what principle, to what final aim these enormous sacrifices have been offered.

— GEORG HEGEL (1770–1831), *Philosophy of History,* 1837

History is a child building a sand castle by the sea, and that child is the whole majesty of man's power in the world.

— HERACLITUS (ca. 535–ca. 475 B.C.), *Herakleitos and Diogenes,* Guy Davenport translation, 1976

History seems to us an arena of instincts and fashions, of appetite, avarice, and craving for power, of blood lust, violence, destruction, and wars, of ambitious ministers, venal generals, bombarded cities, and we too easily forget that this is only one of its many aspects. Above all we forget that we ourselves are a part of history, that we are the product of growth and are condemned to perish if we lose the capacity for further growth and change. We are ourselves history and share the responsibility for world history and our position in it. But we gravely lack awareness of this responsibility.

— HERMANN HESSE (1877–1962), *The Glass Bead Game,* 1943

To study history means submitting to chaos and nevertheless retaining faith in order and meaning. It is a very serious task, young man, and possibly a tragic one.

— HERMANN HESSE (1877–1962), *The Glass Bead Game,* 1943

World history is a court of judgment.
>   — GEORG HEGEL (1770–1831), *The Philosophy of Right*, 1821

I find in the study of history the special discipline which forces me to consider peoples and ages, not my own. . . . It is the most humane of disciplines, and in ways the most humbling. For one cannot ignore those historians of the future who look back on us in the same way.
>   — NATHAN IRVIN HUGGINS (1927–   ), written 1982;
>   quoted in Stanley I. Kutler, ed., *American Retrospectives: Historians on Historians*, 1995

Events in the past may be roughly divided into those which probably never happened and those which do not matter. This is what makes the trade of historian so attractive.
>   — W. R. INGE (1860–1954), *Assessments and Anticipations*, 1929

What are all the records of history but narratives of successive villainies, of treasons and usurpations, massacres and wars?
>   — SAMUEL JOHNSON (1709–1784), *The Rambler*, 175, 1751

"History," Stephen said, "is a nightmare from which I am trying to awake."
>   — JAMES JOYCE, *Portrait of the Artist as a Young Man*, 1916

Who has fully realized that history is not contained in thick books but lives in our very blood?
>   — CARL JUNG (1875–1961), *Woman in Europe*, 1927

History does nothing; it does not possess immense riches, it does not fight battles. It is men, real, living, who do all this. . . . It is not "history" which uses men as a means of achieving—as if it were an individual person—its own ends. History is nothing but the activity of men in pursuit of their ends.
>   — KARL MARX (1818–1883) and FRIEDRICH ENGELS (1820–1895),
>   *The Holy Family*, 1845

What mainly determined the way historians split up history during the past century was a ridiculously adventitious set of circumstances: the way in which public authorities and private persons tended to order the documents which suited their purposes to preserve.

—J. H. HEXTER (1910–1996), *Reappraisals in History*, 1961

History repeats itself, first as tragedy, second as farce.

— KARL MARX (1818–1883), paraphrasing Hegel, in *The Eighteenth Brumaire of Louis Bonaparte*, 1852

Men make their own history, but they do not make it just as they please; they do not make it under circumstances chosen by themselves, but under circumstances directly found, given and transmitted from the past. The tradition of all the dead generations weighs like a nightmare on the brain of the living.

— KARL MARX (1818–1883), *The Eighteenth Brumaire of Louis Bonaparte*, 1852

We know only a single science, the science of history. One can look at history from two sides and divide it into the history of nature and the history of men. However, the two sides are not to be divided off; as long as men exist the history of nature and the history of men are mutually conditioned.

— KARL MARX (1818–1883) and FRIEDRICH ENGELS (1820–1895), *The German Ideology*, 1846

It might never have happened. That's among the most important lessons of history—and of life. There is so much around us that might never have happened were it not for a host of qualities called imagination, commitment, courage, creativity, and determination in the face of obstacles—that maybe most of all.

— DAVID MCCULLOUGH (1933–   ), interview with Roger Mudd, in *Great Minds of History*, 1999

History is the myth, the true myth, of man's fall made manifest in time.

— HENRY MILLER (1891–1980), *Plexus*, 1949

I don't understand anyone who is not interested in history. It's like somebody being color-blind or something. I can't imagine what that's like. And I feel it such a tragedy when people don't know the past. If you tell someone what happened or what somebody was really like and how they got to be where they were, they say, "Well, I never knew that." And it's amazing how many people say to me, "How do you get to the material that's in your books?"—as if nobody has ever told them about going to the library. It's all there.

— DAVID McCULLOUGH (1933–   ), interview with Roger Mudd, in *Great Minds of History,* 1999

History is mostly, it seems to me, a lesson in proportions. You think times are tough? You think you are beset by bad luck? Others have had it worse. Others have gone through worse. Others have triumphed over many more difficult obstacles.

— DAVID McCULLOUGH (1933–   ), interview with Roger Mudd, in *Great Minds of History,* 1999

No, history isn't history. There's no way that we can recapture absolutely, literally, what happened in the past. There's just too much of it, and there are multiple witnesses to what happened in the past.

— JAMES McPHERSON (1943–   ), interview with Roger Mudd, in *Great Minds of History,* 1999

All history is the record of man's single failure to thwart his destiny—the record, in other words, of the few men of destiny who, through the recognition of their symbolic rôle, made history.

— HENRY MILLER (1891–1980), *The Wisdom of the Heart,* 1947

The sociological imagination enables us to grasp history and biography and the relations between the two within society.

— C. WRIGHT MILLS (1916–1962), *The Sociological Imagination,* 1959

Only strong personalities can endure history, the weak ones are extinguished by it.

— FRIEDRICH NIETZSCHE (1844–1900), *Thoughts Out of Season,* 1874

We have need of history in its entirety, not to fall back into it, but to see if we can escape from it.
— José Ortega y Gasset (1883–1955), *The Revolt of the Masses,* 1930

History is written by the winners.
— George Orwell (1903–1950), "As I Please," 1944, in *Shooting an Elephant and Other Essays,* 1950

I believe that history has shape, order, and meaning; that exceptional men, as much as economic forces, produce change; and that passé abstractions like beauty, nobility, and greatness have a shifting but continuing validity.
— Camille Paglia (1947–   ), *Sex, Art, and American Culture,* 1992

What is history? Its beginning is that of the centuries of systematic work devoted to the solution of the enigma of death, so that death itself may eventually be overcome. That is why people write symphonies, and why they discover mathematical infinity and electromagnetic waves.
— Boris Pasternak (1890–1960), *Doctor Zhivago,* 1957

It is one of the basic characteristics of history that the historian is concerned with human beings but that he does not deal with them primarily as individuals, as does the psychologist or the biographer or the novelist. Instead, he deals with them in groups—in religious groups, in cultural groups, in ideological groups, in occupational groups, or in social groups.
— David M. Potter (1910–1971), quoted in David Hackett Fischer, *Historians' Fallacies: Toward a Logic of Historical Thought,* 1970

The subject of history is the gradual realization of all that is practically necessary.
— Friedrich Schlegel (17721829), *Dialogue on Poetry and Literary Aphorisms,* 1798

You have reckoned that history ought to judge the past and to instruct the contemporary world as to the future. The present attempt does not yield to that high office. It will merely tell how it really was.

— LEOPOLD VON RANKE (1795–1886), *History of the Romanic and Germanic Peoples*, 1824

Anyone, however, who has had dealings with dates knows that they are worse than elusive, they are perverse. Events do not happen at the right time, nor in their proper sequence. That sense of harmony with place and season which is so strong in the historian—if he be a readable historian—is lamentably lacking in history, which takes no pains to verify his most convincing statements.

— AGNES REPPLIER (1858–1950), *To Think of Tea!* 1932

History is a great deal closer to poetry than is generally realized; in truth, I think, it is in essence the same.

— A. L. ROWSE (1903–   ), *The Use of History*, 1946

The history of the world and its peoples in three words
"Born,
troubled,
died."

— CARL SANDBURG (1878–1967), *The People, Yes*, 1936

Those who cannot remember the past are condemned to repeat it.

— GEORGE SANTAYANA (1863–1952), *Life of Reason*, 1906

The history of the world is the world's court of justice.

— FRIEDRICH VON SCHILLER (1759–1805), lecture, May 26, 1789

The principle office of history I take to be this: to prevent virtuous actions from being forgotten, and that evil words and deeds should fear an infamous reputation with posterity.

— TACITUS (ca. 55–ca. 120), *The Histories*

The very ink in which history is written is merely fluid prejudice.
— MARK TWAIN (1835–1910), *Following the Equator,* 1897

Science and Technology revolutionize our lives, but memory, tradition and myth frame our response. Expelled from individual consciousness by the rush of change, history finds its revenge by stamping the collective unconscious with habits, values, expectations, dreams. The dialectic between past and future will continue to form our lives.
— ARTHUR SCHLESINGER, JR. (1917–   ), "The Challenge of Change," in *The New York Times Magazine,* July 27, 1986

History is Philosophy teaching by examples.
— THUCYDIDES (ca. 460–ca. 400 B.C.), quoted by Dionysius of Halicarnassus in *Ars Rhetorica*

As soon as histories are properly told there is no more need of romances.
— WALT WHITMAN (1819–1892), Preface to *Leaves of Grass,* 1855

Social history might be defined negatively as the history of a people with the politics left out.
— G. M. TREVELYAN (1876–1962), *English Social History,* 1942

There is nothing new in the world except the history you do not know.
— HARRY S. TRUMAN (1884–1972), in William Hillman, *Mr. President,* 1952

History should be written as philosophy.
— VOLTAIRE (1694–1778), letter, October 31, 1738

A country losing touch with its own history is like an old man losing his glasses, a distressing sight, at once vulnerable, unsure, and easily disoriented.
— GEORGE WALDEN (1939–   ), London *Times,* December 20, 1986

It would strike me as ridiculous to want to doubt the existence of Napoleon; but if someone doubted the existence of the earth 150 years ago, perhaps I should be more willing to listen, for now he is doubting our whole system of evidence.

— LUDWIG WITTGENSTEIN (1889–1951), *On Certainty,* 1961

History not used is nothing, for all intellectual life is action, like practical life, and if you don't use the stuff—well, it might as well be dead.

— A. J. TOYNBEE (1889–1975), television broadcast, April 17, 1955

The one duty we owe to history is to rewrite it.

— OSCAR WILDE (1854–1900), *The Critic as Artist,* 1891

Americans, more than most people, believe that history is the result of individual decisions to implement conscious intentions. For Americans, more than most people, history has been that. This sense of openness, of possibility and autonomy, has been a national asset as precious as the topsoil of the Middle West. But like topsoil, it is subject to erosion; it requires tending. And it is not bad for Americans to come to terms with the fact that for them too, history is a story of inertia and the unforeseen.

— GEORGE F. WILL (1941–   ), *Statecraft as Soulcraft: What Government Does,* 1984

History is not what you thought. *It is what you can remember.* All other history defeats itself.

— W. C. SELLAR (1898–1951) and R. J. YEATMAN (1897–1968), *1066 and All That,* 1930

What has history to do with me? Mine is the first and only world! I want to report how I find the world. What others have told me about the world is a very small and incidental part of my experience. I have to judge the world, to measure things.

— LUDWIG WITTGENSTEIN (1889–1951), 1915 entry in *Notebooks 1914–1916*

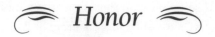

Honor

I sighed as a lover, I obeyed as a son.
— EDWARD GIBBON (1737–1794), *Memoirs of My Life,* 1796

A prince never lacks legitimate reasons to break his promise.
— NICCOLÒ MACHIAVELLI (1469–1527), *The Prince,* 1514

It is the dissimilarities and inequalities among men which give rise
to the notion of honor; as such differences become less, it grows
feeble; and when they disappear, it will vanish too.
— ALEXIS DE TOCQUEVILLE (1805–1859), *Democracy in America,*
1840

Honor wears different coats to different eyes.
— BARBARA TUCHMAN (1912–1989), *The Guns of August,* 1962

There is no question what the roll of honor in America is. The roll
of honor consists of the names of men who have squared their conduct by ideals of duty.
— WOODROW WILSON (1856–1924), speech, February 27, 1916

Human Nature and
the Human Condition

Man is a singular creature. He has a set of gifts which make him
unique among the animals: so that, unlike them, he is not a figure
in the landscape—he is a shaper of the landscape.
— JACOB BRONOWSKI (1908–1974), *The Ascent of Man,* 1973

The present life of man, O king, seems to me, in comparison of that time which is unknown to us, like the swift flight of a sparrow through the room wherein you sit at supper in winter, with your commanders and ministers, and a good fire in the midst, whilst the storms of rain and snow prevail abroad; the sparrow, I say, flying in at one door, and immediately out at another, whilst he is within, is safe from the wintry storm; but after a short space of fair weather, he immediately vanishes out of your sight, into the dark winter from which he had emerged. So this life of man appears for a short space, but of what went before, or what is to follow, we are utterly ignorant.

➤ VENERABLE BEDE (ca. 672–ca. 735), *Ecclesiastical History of the English People*

What a man is ashamed of is always at bottom himself; and he is ashamed of himself at bottom always for being afraid.

➤ R. G. COLLINGWOOD (1889–1943), *The New Leviathan*, 1942

I have found little that is "good" about human beings on the whole. In my experience most of them are trash, no matter whether they publicly subscribe to this or that ethical doctrine or to none at all. That is something that you cannot say aloud, or perhaps even think.

➤ SIGMUND FREUD (1856–1939), letter, October 9, 1918

We are human because, at a very early stage in the history of our species, our ancestors discovered a way of preserving and disseminating the results of experience.

➤ ALDOUS HUXLEY (1894–1963), *Tomorrow and Tomorrow and Tomorrow and Other Essays*, 1956

It is only too clear that man is not at home in this universe, and yet he is not good enough to deserve a better.

➤ PERRY MILLER (1905–1963), *The New England Mind: The Seventeenth Century*, 1939

I teach you the Superman [Übermensch]. Man is something that should be overcome.

➤ FRIEDRICH NIETZSCHE (1844–1900), *Thus Spoke Zarathustra*, 1884

Man is no longer an artist, he has become a work of art.
— FRIEDRICH NIETZSCHE (1844–1900), *The Birth of Tragedy,* 1872

The belly is the reason why man does not mistake himself for a god.
— FRIEDRICH NIETZSCHE (1844–1900), *Beyond Good and Evil,* 1886

Instinct. When the house burns, one forgets even lunch. Yes, but one eats it later in the ashes.
— FRIEDRICH NIETZSCHE (1844–1900), *Beyond Good and Evil,* 1886

For human nature is as surely made arrogant by consideration as it is awed by firmness.
— THUCYDIDES (ca. 460–400 B.C.), *The History of the Peloponnesian War*

Hype and Skepticism

Nearly everything we do to enlarge our world, to make life more interesting, more varied, more exciting, more vivid, more "fabulous," more promising, in the long run has the opposite effect.
— DANIEL J. BOORSTIN (1914–   ), *The Image: A Guide to Pseudo-Events in America,* 1961

It is only a short step from exaggerating what we can find in the world to exaggerating our power to remake the world. Expecting more novelty than there is, more greatness than there is, and more strangeness than there is, we imagine ourselves masters of a plastic universe. But a world we can shape to our will . . . is a shapeless world.
— DANIEL J. BOORSTIN (1914–   ), *The Image: A Guide to Pseudo-Events in America,* 1961

We read advertisements . . . to discover and enlarge our desires. We are always ready—even eager—to discover, from the announcement of a new product, what we have all along wanted without really knowing it.

— DANIEL J. BOORSTIN (1914–   ), *The Image: A Guide to Pseudo-Events in America,* 1961

In fast-moving, progress-conscious America, the consumer expects to be dizzied by progress. If he could completely understand advertising jargon, he would be badly disappointed. The half-intelligibility which we expect, or even hope, to find in the latest product language personally reassures each of us that progress *is* being made: that the pace exceeds our ability to follow.

— DANIEL J. BOORSTIN (1914–   ), *The Image: A Guide to Pseudo-Events in America,* 1961

The deeper problems connected with advertising come less from the unscrupulousness of our "deceivers" than from our pleasure in being deceived, less from the desire to seduce than from the desire to be seduced.

— DANIEL J. BOORSTIN (1914–   ), *The Image: A Guide to Pseudo-Events in America,* 1961

A modern dictator with the resources of science at his disposal can easily lead the public on from day to day, destroying all persistency of thought and aim, so that memory is blurred by the multiplicity of daily news and judgment baffled by its perversion.

— WINSTON CHURCHILL (1874–1965), *The Second World War,* 1959

Scepticism, as I said, is not intellectual only; it is moral also; a chronic atrophy and disease of the whole soul. A man lives by believing something; not by debating and arguing about many things. A sad case for him when all that he can manage to believe is something he can button in his pocket, and with one or the other organ eat and digest! Lower than that he will not get.

— THOMAS CARLYLE (1795–1881), *On Heroes, Hero-Worship, and the Heroic in History,* 1841

When the gods wish to punish us, they make us believe our own advertising.

➤ DANIEL J. BOORSTIN (1914–), *The Image: A Guide to Pseudo-Events in America*, 1961

It is no great art to say something briefly when, like Tacitus, one has something to say; when one has nothing to say, however, and nonetheless writes a whole book and makes truth . . . into a liar—that I call an achievement.

➤ G. C. LICHTENBERG (1742–1799), *Aphorisms*, 1799

Advertising is the greatest art form of the twentieth century.

➤ MARSHALL MCLUHAN (1911–1980), in *Advertising Age*, September 3, 1976

Ideally, advertising aims at the goal of a programmed harmony among all human impulses and aspirations and endeavors. Using handicraft methods, it stretches out toward the ultimate electronic goal of a collective consciousness.

➤ MARSHALL MCLUHAN (1911–1980), *Understanding Media*, 1964

Today the tyrant rules not by club or fist, but, disguised as a market researcher, he shepherds his flocks in the ways of utility and comfort.

➤ MARSHALL MCLUHAN (1911–1980), *The Mechanical Bride*, 1951

When producers want to know what the public wants, they graph it as curves. When they want to tell the public what to get, they say it in curves.

➤ MARSHALL MCLUHAN (1911–1980), *The Mechanical Bride*, 1951

 Ideals and Idealism

The destiny of mankind is not decided by material computation.
— WINSTON CHURCHILL (1874–1965), radio broadcast, June 16, 1941

Amid the pressure of great events, a general principle gives no help.
— GEORG HEGEL (1770–1831), *The Philosophy of History*, 1837

The idealist is incorrigible: if he is thrown out of his heaven, he makes an ideal of his hell.
— FRIEDRICH NIETZSCHE (1844–1900), *Miscellaneous Maxims and Opinions*, 1879

. . . nations generally, like people, have the kind of ideals which they can afford, and . . . we [Americans] had the good fortune to be able to afford some rather expensive ideals.
— DAVID POTTER (1910–1971), interview in John Garraty, ed., *Interpreting American History*, 1970

The ideal was a vision of order maintained by the warrior class and formulated in the image of the Round Table, nature's perfect shape. King Arthur's knights adventured for the right against dragons, enchanters, and wicked men, establishing order in a wild world. So their living counterparts [the knights of medieval Europe] were supposed, in theory, to serve as defenders of the Faith, upholders of justice, champions of the oppressed. In practice, they were themselves the oppressors, and by the 14th century the violence and lawlessness of men of the sword had become a major agency of disorder. When the gap between ideal and real becomes too wide, the system breaks down.
— BARBARA TUCHMAN (1912–1989), *A Distant Mirror: The Calamitous 14th Century*, 1978

Many have dreamed up republics and principalities that have never in truth been known to exist; the gulf between how one should live and how one does live is so wide that a man who neglects what is actually done for what should be done learns the way to self-destruction rather than self-preservation.

— NICCOLÒ MACHIAVELLI (1469–1527), *The Prince*, 1514

Anyone who seeks to destroy the passions instead of controlling them is trying to play the angel.

— VOLTAIRE (1694–1778), *Letters on England*, 1732

Ignorance

Nothing in education is so astonishing as the amount of ignorance it accumulates in the form of inert facts.

— HENRY BROOK ADAMS (1838–1918), in Laurence J. Peter, *Peter's Quotations*, 1977

The greatest obstacle to discovery is not ignorance—it is the illusion of knowledge.

— DANIEL J. BOORSTIN (1914–   ), quoted in Carol Krucoff, "The 6 O'Clock Scholar," *The Washington Post*, January 29, 1984

I do not believe in the collective wisdom of individual ignorance.

— THOMAS CARLYLE (1795–1881), *The Age of Reason*, 1794

Immigrants

So Europe watched them go—in less than a century and a half, well over thirty-five million of them from every part of the continent. In this common flow were gathered up peoples of the most diverse qualities, people whose rulers had for centuries been enemies, people who had not even known of each other's existence. Now they would share each other's future.

— OSCAR HANDLIN (1915–   ), *The Uprooted: The Epic Story of the Great Migrations That Made the American People,* 1951

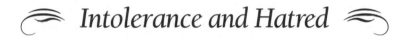

Intolerance and Hatred

Xenophobia looks like it is becoming the mass ideology of the 20th-century *fin-de-siècle*. What holds humanity together today is the denial of what the human race has in common.

— ERIC HOBSBAWM (1917–   ), lecture published in *Anthropology Today,* February 1992

It is human nature to hate the man whom you have hurt.

— TACITUS (ca. 55–ca. 120 A.D.), *Agricola*

As the global expansion of Indian and Chinese restaurants suggests, xenophobia is directed against foreign people, not foreign cultural imports.

— ERIC HOBSBAWM (1917–   ), lecture published in *Anthropology Today,* February 1992

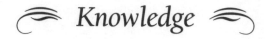

Knowledge

Science fiction writers foresee the inevitable, and although problems and catastrophes may be inevitable, solutions are not.
— Isaac Asimov (1920–1992), "How Easy to See the Future," *Natural History,* 1975

I don't pretend to understand the Universe—it's a great deal bigger than I am.
— Thomas Carlyle (1795–1881), spoken 1868, quoted in William Allingham, *A Diary,* 1907

A man ceases to be a beginner in any given science and becomes a master in that science when he has learned that . . . he is going to be a beginner all his life.
— R. G. Collingwood (1889–1943), *The New Leviathan,* 1942

The dawn of knowledge is usually the false dawn.
— Bernard De Voto (1897–1955), *The Course of Empire,* 1952

We do not need to be shoemakers to know if our shoes fit, and just as little have we any need to be professionals to acquire knowledge of matters of universal interest.
— Georg Hegel (1770–1831), *The Philosophy of Right,* 1821

The learner always begins by finding fault, but the scholar sees the positive merit in everything.
— Georg Hegel (1770–1831), *The Philosophy of Right,* 1821

Logicians may reason about abstractions. But the great mass of men must have images. The strong tendency of the multitude in all ages and nations to idolatry can be explained on no other principle.
— Thomas Babington Macaulay (1800–1859), "Milton," 1825, reprinted in *Critical and Historical Essays,* 1843

If we do discover a [unified field theory explaining the universe], it should in time be understandable in broad principle by everyone, not just a few scientists. Then we shall all . . . be able to take part in the discussion of the question of why it is that we and the universe exist. If we find the answer to that, it would be the ultimate triumph of human reason—for then we should know the mind of God.

— STEPHEN HAWKING (1942–   ), *A Brief History of Time*, 1988

Natural science will in time incorporate into itself the science of man, just as the science of man will incorporate into itself natural science: there will be one science.

— KARL MARX (1818–1883), *Economic and Philosophic Manuscripts of 1844*, translated and published, 1964

The product of mental labor—science—always stands far below its value, because the labor-time necessary to reproduce it has no relation at all to the labor-time required for its original production.

— KARL MARX (1818–1883), *Theories of Surplus Value*, 1863

Does wisdom perhaps appear on the earth as a raven which is inspired by the smell of carrion?

— FRIEDRICH NIETZSCHE (1844–1900), *Twilight of the Idols*, 1889

Our treasure lies in the beehive of our knowledge. We are perpetually on the way thither, being by nature winged insects and honey gatherers of the mind.

— FRIEDRICH NIETZSCHE (1844–1900), *The Genealogy of Morals*, 1887

We have no organ at all for *knowledge*, for "truth": we "know" (or believe or imagine) precisely as much as may be useful in the interest of the human herd, the species: and even what is here called "usefulness" is in the end only a belief, something imagined and perhaps precisely that most fatal piece of stupidity by which we shall one day perish.

— FRIEDRICH NIETZSCHE (1844–1900), *The Gay Science*, 1887

Science may be described as the art of systematic over-simplification.
— KARL POPPER (1902–   ), quoted in London *Observer*, August 1,
1982

Knowledge is the most democratic source of power.
— ALVIN TOFFLER (1928–   ), *Powershift: Knowledge, Wealth, and
Violence at the Edge of the 21st Century*, 1990

Only by strict specialization can the scientific worker become fully
conscious, for once and perhaps never again in his lifetime, that he
has achieved something that will endure. A really definitive and
good accomplishment is today always a specialized accomplishment. And whoever lacks the capacity to put on blinders, so to
speak, and to come up to the idea that the fate of his soul depends
upon whether or not he makes the correct conjecture at this pas-
sage of this manuscript may as well stay away from science. He will
never have what one may call the "personal experience" of science.
Without this strange intoxication, ridiculed by every outsider;
without this passion . . . you have *no* calling for science and you
should do something else. For nothing is worthy of man as man
unless he can pursue it with passionate devotion.
— MAX WEBER (1864–1920), *Essays in Sociology*, 1919

The effort to understand the universe is one of the very few things
that lifts human life a little above the level of farce, and gives it
some of the grace of tragedy.
— STEVEN WEINBERG (1933–   ), *The First Three Minutes: A Modern View of the Origin of the Universe*, 1977

Leaders

[The American President] resembles the commander of a ship at sea. He must have a helm to grasp, a course to steer, a port to seek.
— HENRY BROOK ADAMS (1838–1918), *The Education of Henry Adams,* 1907

Nobody trusted Dick Nixon. Nixon wasn't looking for people to like him. And Nixon wasn't really looking for people to trust him. Nixon was looking for power.
— STEPHEN AMBROSE, interview with Roger Mudd, in *Great Minds of History,* 1999

I very often get asked, "What's the secret of leadership?" My only answer to that is, "I'm damned if I know, because they all have different ways. MacArthur's way was certainly different from Eisenhower's, which was certainly different from Nixon's, which was certainly different from Churchill's, and you can go on and on with that.
But there's one quality that all great men share, and that's luck. Napoleon spoke to that. He was asked what qualities he was looking for his generals, and he said, just one—that they be lucky. Well Jimmy Carter was unlucky. And, in a lot of ways, I think Bill Clinton is unlucky. Peace and prosperity can't compare to war and destruction and making decisions that affect the whole world.
— STEPHEN AMBROSE (1936–   ), interview with Roger Mudd, in *Great Minds of History,* 1999

[General George C. Marshall] did not feel it necessary to praise others. A man knew that he had met the Chief of Staff's expectations when he received increased responsibility and the rank that went with it.
— STEPHEN AMBROSE (1936–   ), "George C. Marshall," *American History Illustrated,* February 1970

He saw Mr. Lincoln but once; at the melancholy function called an Inaugural Ball. Of course he looked anxiously for a sign of character. He saw a long, awkward figure; a plain, ploughed face; a mind, absent in part, and in part evidently worried by white kid gloves; features that expressed neither self-satisfaction nor any other familiar Americanism, but rather the same painful sense of becoming educated and of needing education that tormented a private secretary, above all a lack of apparent force. Any private secretary in the least fit for his business would have thought, as Adams did, that no man living needed so much education as the new President but that all the education he could get would not be enough.

— HENRY BROOK ADAMS (1838–1918), *The Education of Henry Adams*, 1907

Throughout the War I deliberately avoided intervening in a subordinate's duties. When an officer performed as I expected him to, I gave him a free hand. When he hesitated, I tried to help him. And when he failed, I relieved him.

— OMAR N. BRADLEY (1893–1981), *A Soldier's Story*, 1951

If Hitler invaded hell, I would make at least a favourable reference to the devil in the House of Commons.

— WINSTON CHURCHILL (1874–1965), *The History of the Second World War: The Grand Alliance*, 1950

All Presidents start out to run a crusade but after a couple of years they find they are running something less heroic and much more intractable: namely the Presidency. The people are well cured by then of election fever, during which they think they are choosing Moses. In the third year, they look on the man as a sinner and a bumbler and begin to poke around for rumours of another Messiah.

— ALISTAIR COOKE (1908–), *Talk About America*, 1968

No President can be a prisoner of his staff unless he chooses to be.

— EDWIN C. HARGROVE (1930–) *Presidential Leadership: Personality and Political Style*, 1966

Europeans often ask, and Americans do not always explain, how it happens that this great office [of the President] . . . is not more frequently filled by great and striking men.

—JAMES BRYCE (1838–1922), *The American Commonwealth,* 1888

[Robert E. Lee's] aversion to personal confrontation . . . became his greatest weakness as a military commander.

—JOHN EISENHOWER (1922–   ), "The Commander," *New York Times Book Review,* August 6, 1995

Of the many confused scuffles it has been my professional pleasure to study, the one that ensued [when Franklin Roosevelt met with Herbert Hoover on January 20, 1933] is the hardest to relate with confident accuracy. It was reminiscent of a naval engagement on a foggy night between two opposed fleets, each ship firing a gun whenever a flash was seen, being quite as likely to blow up a friend as an enemy. In this instance as well, the proponents were shooting at shadows and hitting the air.

—HERBERT FEIS (1893–1872), *1933: Characters in Crisis,* 1966

Churchill is the very type of a corrupt journalist. There is not a worse prostitute in politics. He himself has written that it's unimaginable what can be done in war with the help of lies. He's an utterly amoral repulsive creature. I'm convinced that he has his place of refuge ready beyond the Atlantic. He obviously won't seek sanctuary in Canada. In Canada he'd be beaten up. He'll go to his friends the Yankees. As soon as this damnable winter is over, we'll remedy all that.

—ADOLF HITLER (1889–1945), in conversation with General Erwin Rommel, February 18, 1942

The answer to the runaway Presidency is not the messenger-boy Presidency. The American democracy must discover a middle ground between making the President a czar and making him a puppet.

—ARTHUR SCHLESINGER, JR. (1917–   ), *The Imperial Presidency,* 1973

A multitude of rulers is not a good thing. Let there be one ruler, one king.
— HOMER (lived 8th century, B.C.), *Iliad*

In every age the vilest specimens of human nature are to be found among demagogues.
— THOMAS BABINGTON MACAULAY (1800–1859), *History of England,* 1849

One must never be drawn off the job in hand by the gratuitous advice from those who are not fully in the operational picture, and who have no responsibility.
— BERNARD LAW MONTGOMERY (1887–1976), *Memoirs of Field Marshall Montgomery,* 1958

The most dangerous follower is he whose defection would destroy the whole party: that is to say, the best follower.
— FRIEDRICH NIETZSCHE (1844–1900), *The Wanderer and His Shadow,* 1880

[Caesar] slept generally in his chariots or litters, employing even his rest in pursuit of action.
— PLUTARCH (before 50–after 120), *Parallel Lives*

Thus in the highest position there is the least freedom of action.
— SALLUST (86–34 B.C.), *The War with Cataline*

Brave men earn the right to shape their own destiny.
— ARTHUR SCHLESINGER, JR. (1917–   ), *Saturday Evening Post,* November 1, 1958

No man can properly command an army from the rear, he must be "at its front"; and when a detachment is made, the commander thereof should be informed of the object to be accomplished, and left as free as possible to execute it in his own way.
— WILLIAM TECUMSEH SHERMAN (1820–1891), *Memoirs of General W. T. Sherman,* 1891

[Of the Emperor Galba:] No one would have doubted his ability to reign had he never been emperor.
  ➤ TACITUS (ca. 55–ca. 120), *The Histories*

[Of British World War II general Harold Alexander:] Perfect soldier, perfect gentleman . . . never gave offence to anyone, not even the enemy.
  ➤ A. J. P. TAYLOR (1906–1990), letter, March 16, 1973

If, in looking at the lives of princes, courtiers, men of rank and fashion, we must perforce depict them as idle, profligate, and criminal, we must make allowances for the rich men's failings, and recollect that we, too, were very likely indolent and voluptuous, had we no motive for work, a mortal's natural taste for pleasure and the daily temptation of a large income.
  ➤ WILLIAM MAKEPEACE THACKERAY (1811–1863), *The Four Georges*, 1855

Whenever [Pericles] saw [his troops] unseasonably and insolently elated, he would reduce them to alarm; on the other hand, if they fell victims to a panic, he could at once restore them to confidence.
  ➤ THUCYDIDES (460?–400? B.C.), *The Peloponnesian War*

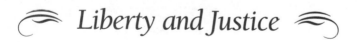

⌒ *Liberty and Justice* ⌒

The most certain test by which we judge whether a country is really free is the amount of security enjoyed by minorities.
  ➤ LORD ACTON (1834–1902), "The History of Freedom in Antiquity," 1877, in *The History of Freedom and Other Essays*, 1907

Liberty is not a means to a higher political end. It is itself the highest political end.
  ➤ LORD ACTON (1834–1902), Introduction, *The History of Freedom and Other Essays*, 1907

Only through human freedom and responsibility are history and salvation able to fulfill themselves.

— LEO BAECK (1873–1956), *The Essence of Judaism*, 1936

The liberty of the individual is no gift of civilization. It was greatest before there was any civilization.

— SIGMUND FREUD (1856–1939), *Civilization and Its Discontents*, 1930

The East knew and to the present day knows only that *One* is Free; the Greek and the Roman world, that *Some* are free; the German World knows that *All* are free. The first political form therefore which we observe in History is *Despotism*, the second *Democracy* and *Aristocracy*, the third *Monarchy*.

— GEORG HEGEL (1770–1831), *The Philosophy of History*, 1837

The history of the world is none other than the progress of the consciousness of freedom.

— GEORG HEGEL (1770–1831), *The Philosophy of History*, 1837

When liberty is mentioned, we must always be careful to observe whether it is not really the assertion of private interests which is thereby designated.

— GEORG HEGEL (1770–1831), *The Philosophy of History*, 1837

Man's capacity for justice makes democracy possible, but man's inclination to injustice makes democracy necessary.

— REINHOLD NIEBUHR (1892–1971), *The Children of Light and the Children of Darkness*, 1944

How is freedom measured, in individuals as in nations? By the resistance which has to be overcome, by the effort it costs to stay *aloft*. One would have to seek the highest type of free man where the greatest resistance is constantly being overcome: five steps from tyranny, near the threshold of the danger of servitude.

— FRIEDRICH NIETZSCHE (1844–1900), *Twilight of the Idols*, 1889

Everyone ought to worship God according to his own inclinations, and not to be constrained by force.

— FLAVIUS JOSEPHUS (37–95?), *Life of Flavius Josephus*

It is the rare fortune of these days that one may think what one likes and say what one thinks.

— TACITUS (ca. 55–ca. 120), *The Histories*

In America the majority raises formidable barriers around the liberty of opinion; within these barriers an author may write what he pleases, but woe to him if he goes beyond them.

— ALEXIS DE TOCQUEVILLE (1805–1859), *Democracy in America,* 1840

Scarcely any political question arises in the United States that is not resolved, sooner or later, into a judicial question.

— ALEXIS DE TOCQUEVILLE (1805–1859), *Democracy in America,* 1840

The best laws cannot make a constitution work in spite of morals; morals can turn the worst laws to advantage. That is a commonplace truth, but one to which my studies are always bringing me back. It is the central point in my conception. I see it at the end of all my reflections.

— ALEXIS DE TOCQUEVILLE (1805–1859), *Democracy in America,* 1835–1840

I disapprove of what you say, but I will defend to the death your right to say it.

— VOLTAIRE (1694–1778), popular paraphrase from Voltaire's *Essay on Tolerance*

∊ Logic and Reason ∍

We have long since learned not to bother overmuch with reason and logic. Logic was formerly visualized as something outside us, something existing independently which, if we were willing, could take us by the hand and lead us into the paths of truth. We now suspect that it was something the mind has created to conceal its timidity and keep up its courage, a hocus-pocus designed to give formal validity to conclusions we're willing to accept if everybody else in our set will too. If all men are mortal (an assumption), and Socrates was a man (in the sense assumed), no doubt Socrates must have been mortal; but we suspect that we somehow knew all this before it was submitted to the test of a syllogism. Logics have a way of multiplying in response to the changes in point of view. The secure foundations of deductive and inductive logic have been battered to pieces by the ascertainable facts, so that we really have no choice; we must cling to the ascertainable facts though they slay us.

— CARL BECKER (1873–1945), *The Heavenly City of the Eighteenth-Century Philosophers,* 1932

We find nothing easier than being wise, patient, superior. We drip with the oil of forbearance and sympathy, we are absurdly just, we forgive everything. For that very reason we ought to discipline ourselves a little; for that very reason we ought to *cultivate* a little emotion, a little emotional vice, from time to time. It may be hard for us; and among ourselves we may perhaps laugh at the appearance we thus present. But what of that! We no longer have any other mode of self-overcoming available to us: this is *our* asceticism, *our* penance.

— FRIEDRICH NIETZSCHE (1844–1900), *Twilight of the Idols,* 1889

Fanatics are picturesque, mankind would rather see gestures than listen to *reasons.*

— FRIEDRICH NIETZSCHE (1844–1900), *The Anti-Christ,* 1895

Marxists and Freudians, in their different ways, have taught us all to look for nonrational causes for ideas and beliefs which on the surface look perfectly rational, and have convinced some that rational thinking as such is an impossibility. But though we cannot (and should not) return to the naive confidence of our grandfathers in these matters, it must nonetheless be pointed out that the antirationalist case here cannot be stated without contradiction. It undermined not only the theories of which its proponents disapprove, but itself as well. For it asks us to believe, as a matter of rational conviction, that rational conviction is impossible. And this we cannot do.

— W. H. WALSH (1913–1986), *Philosophy of History,* 1960

Thomas Babington Macaulay

His enemies might have said before that he talked rather too much; but now he has occasional flashes of silence, that make his conversation perfectly delightful.

— SYDNEY SMITH (1771–1845), in Lady Holland, *Memoir,* 1855

Marxism

Much of the world's work, it has been said, is done by men who do not feel quite well. Marx is a case in point.

— JOHN KENNETH GALBRAITH (1908–   ), *The Age of Uncertainty,* 1977

All I know is I'm not a Marxist.

— KARL MARX (1818–1883), quoted by Friedrich Engels in a letter, August 5, 1890

Marxism is the opium of the intellectuals.

— EDMUND WILSON (1895–1972), *Letters on Literature and Politics*, 1977

Misery

Man's unhappiness, as I construe, comes of his greatness; it is because there is an Infinite in him, which with all his cunning he cannot quite bury under the Finite.

— THOMAS CARLYLE (1795–1881), *Sartor Resartus*, 1836

Our sympathy is cold to the relation of distant misery.

— EDWARD GIBBON (1737–1794), *The Decline and Fall of the Roman Empire*, 1776–1788

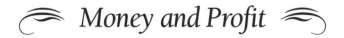

Money and Profit

A generation which has passed through the shop has absorbed standards and ambitions which are not of those of spaciousness, and cannot get away from them. Everything with them is done as though for sale, and they naturally have in view the greatest possible benefit, profit and that end of the stuff that will make the best show.

— ALEXANDER HERZEN (1812–1870), *My Past and Thoughts*, 1921

Cash-payment never was, or could except for a few years be, the union-bond of man to man. Cash never yet paid one man fully his deserts to another; nor could it, nor can it, now or henceforth to the end of the world.

—Thomas Carlyle (1795–1881), *Past and Present,* 1843

One can relish the varied idiocy of human action during a [financial] panic to the full, for, while it is a time of great tragedy, nothing is being lost but money.

—John Kenneth Galbraith (1908–   ), *The Great Crash, 1929,* 1955

Landlords, like all other men, love to reap where they never sowed.

—Karl Marx (1818–1883), *Early Writings,* 1884

While the miser is merely a capitalist gone mad, the capitalist is a rational miser.

—Karl Marx (1818–1883), *Capital,* 1867

All social rules and all relations between individuals are eroded by a cash economy, avarice drags Pluto himself out of the bowels of the earth.

—Kari Marx (1818–1883), *Capital,* 1867

Money is a poor man's credit card.

—Marshall McLuhan (1911–1980), in *Maclean's,* June 1971

[Skyscrapers:] The sardonic funeral towers of metropolitan finance.

—Lewis Mumford (1895–1990), *The Culture of Cities,* 1938

As one digs deeper into the national character of the Americans, one sees that they have sought the value of everything in this world only in the answer to this single question: how much money will it bring in?

—Alexis de Tocqueville (1805–1859), letter, June 9, 1831

In no other country in the world is the love of property keener or more alert than in the United States, and nowhere else does the majority display less inclination toward doctrines which in any way threaten the way property is owned.

━ ALEXIS DE TOCQUEVILLE (1805–1859), *Democracy in America,* 1840

 *Morality*

If you can impress any man with an absorbing conviction of the supreme importance of some moral or religious doctrine; if you can make him believe that those who reject that doctrine are doomed to eternal perdition; if you then give that man power, and by means of his ignorance blind him to the ulterior consequences of his own act—he will infallibly persecute those who deny his doctrine; and the extent of his persecution will be regulated by the extent of his sincerity.

━ HENRY THOMAS BUCKLE (1821–1862), *History of Civilization in England,* 1858

I love treason but hate a traitor.

━ JULIUS CAESAR (100–44 B.C.), in Plutarch, *Lives*

For the "superior morality," of which we hear so much, we too would desire to be thankful: at the same time, it were but blindness to deny that this "superior morality" is properly rather an "inferior criminality," produced not by greater love of Virtue, but by greater perfection of Police; and of that far subtler and stronger Police, called Public Opinion.

━ THOMAS CARLYLE (1795–1881), *Signs of the Times,* 1838

Man arose to high moral vision two thousand years before the Hebrew nation was born.

━ JAMES HENRY BREASTED (1865–1935), *The Dawn of Conscience,* 1933

Caught in the relaxing interval between one moral code and the next, an unmoored generation surrenders itself to luxury, corruption, and a restless disorder of family and friends.
— WILL and ARIEL DURANT, in Lewis H. Lapham, "In the Garden of Tabloid Delights," *Harper's*, August 1997

To deny freedom of the will is to make morality impossible.
— JAMES A. FROUDE (1818–1894), "Calvinism," in *Short Studies on Great Subjects*, 1883

The man who does evil to another does evil to himself.
— HESIOD (8TH CENTURY B.C.), *WORKS AND DAYS*

There is not much that even the most socially responsible scientists can do as individuals, or even as a group, about the social consequences of their activities.
— ERIC HOBSBAWM (1917–   ), *New York Review of Books*, November 19, 1970

We know no spectacle so ridiculous as the British public in one of its periodical fits of morality.
— THOMAS BABINGTON MACAULAY (1800–1859), "Moore's *Life of Lord Byron*," 1831, reprinted in *Critical and Historical Essays*, 1843

Again and again I am brought up against it, and again and again I resist it: I don't want to believe it, even though it is almost palpable: *the vast majority lack an intellectual conscience;* indeed, it often seems to me that to demand such a thing is to be in the most populous cities as solitary as in the desert.
— FRIEDRICH NIETZSCHE (1844–1900), *The Gay Science*, 1887

What is good? All that heightens the feeling of power, the will to power, power itself in man.
— FRIEDRICH NIETZSCHE (1844–1900), *The Anti-Christ*, 1895

What was the meaning of that South Sea Exploring Expedition, with all its parade and expense, but an indirect recognition of the fact, that there are continents and seas in the moral world, to which every man is an isthmus or an inlet, yet unexplored by him, but that it is easier to sail many thousand miles through cold and storm and cannibals, in a government ship, with five hundred men and boys to assist one, than it is to explore the private sea, the Atlantic and the Pacific Ocean of one's being alone.

⟶ HENRY DAVID THOREAU (1817–1862), *Walden*, 1854

We have been God-like in our planned breeding of our domesticated plants and animals, but we have been rabbit-like in our unplanned breeding of ourselves.

⟶ A. J. TOYNBEE (1889–1975), in *National Observer*, June 10, 1963

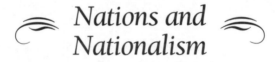

Nations and Nationalism

The true courage of civilized nations is readiness for sacrifice in the service of the state, so that the individual counts as only one amongst many. The important thing here is not personal mettle but aligning oneself with the universal.

⟶ GEORG HEGEL (1770–1831), *The Philosophy of Right*, 1821

The essence of the modern state is that the universal be bound up with the complete freedom of its particular members and with private well-being, that thus the interests of family and civil society must concentrate themselves on the state. . . . It is only when both these moments subsist in their strength that the state can be regarded as articulated and genuinely organized.

⟶ GEORG HEGEL (1770–1831), *The Philosophy of Right*, 1821

As high as mind stands above nature, so high does the state stand above physical life. Man must therefore venerate the state as a secular deity. . . . The march of God in the world, that is what the State is.
— GEORG HEGEL (1770–1831), *The Philosophy of Right*, 1821

If nations always moved from one set of furnished rooms to another—and always into a better set—things might be easier, but the trouble is that there is no one to prepare the new rooms. The future is worse than the ocean—there is nothing there. It will be what men and circumstances make it.
— ALEXANDER HERZEN (1812–1870), *From the Other Shore*, 1849

Nations without a past are contradictions in terms. What makes a nation *is* the past, what justifies one nation against others is the past, and historians are the people who produce it.
— ERIC HOBSBAWM (1917–   ), lecture to the American Anthropological Association, published in *Anthropology Today*, 1992

States that rise quickly, just as all the other things of nature that are born and grow rapidly, cannot have roots and ramifications; the first bad weather kills them.
— NICCOLÒ MACHIAVELLI (1469–1527), *The Prince*, 1514

It is true that men themselves made this world of nations . . . but this world without doubt has issued from a mind often diverse, at times quite contrary, and always superior to the particular ends that men had proposed to themselves.
— GIAMBATTISTA VICO (1688–1744), *The New Science*, 1744

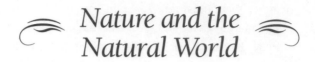

Nature and the Natural World

It is interesting to contemplate an entangled bank, clothed with many plants of many kinds, with birds singing on the bushes, with various insects flitting about, and with worms crawling through the damp earth, and to reflect that these elaborately constructed forms, so different from each other, and dependent on each other in so complex a manner, have all been produced by laws acting around us.
 ⤙ CHARLES DARWIN (1809–1882), *On the Origin of Species,* 1859

When the views advanced by me in this volume . . . are generally admitted, we can dimly foresee that there will be a considerable revolution in natural history.
 ⤙ CHARLES DARWIN (1809–1882), *On the Origin of Species,* 1859

Ontogenesis, or the development of the individual, is a short and quick recapitulation of phylogenesis, or the development of the tribe to which it belongs, determined by the laws of inheritance and adaptation.
 ⤙ ERNST HEINRICH HAECKEL (1834–1919), *The History of Creation,* 1868

According to the best authorities, the world in which we dwell is a huge, opaque, inanimate mass floating in the vast ethereal ocean of infinite space. It has the form of an orange, being an oblate spheroid, curiously flattened at opposite parts for the insertion of two imaginary poles which are supposed to penetrate and unite at the center; thus forming an axis on which the mighty orange turns with a regular diurnal revolution.
 ⤙ WASHINGTON IRVING (1783–1859), *Knickerbocker's History of New York,* 1809

The world began without the human race and it will end without it.
 ⤙ CLAUDE LÉVI-STRAUSS (1908–   ), *Tristes Tropiques,* 1955

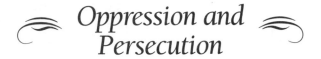

Oppression and Persecution

The colonized races, those slaves of modern times, are impatient.
— FRANTZ FANON (1925–1961), *The Wretched of the Earth*, 1961

As for those who were torn away to America [as slaves], none would have willed it so. None, beforehand, could have imagined the awful agony to be endured—the separation from all that they were, the voyage into empty space, the trials of adjustment to a new life. Rudely forced, they were, nevertheless, destined to help create a new world, to become the founding fathers and mothers of a new people.
— NATHAN IRVING HUGGINS (1927–   ), *Black Odyssey: The African-American Ordeal in Slavery*, 1977

Almost everything we call "higher culture" is based on the spiritualization and intensification of *cruelty*—this is my proposition. . . . That which constitutes the painful voluptuousness of tragedy is cruelty; that which produces a pleasing effect in so-called tragic pity, indeed fundamentally in everything sublime up to the most highest and most refined thrills of metaphysics, derives its sweetness solely from the ingredient of cruelty mixed in with it.
— FRIEDRICH NIETZSCHE (1844–1900), *Beyond Good and Evil*, 1886

Machines were, it may be said, the weapon employed by the capitalists to quell the revolt of specialized labor.
— KARL MARX (1818–1883), *The Poverty of Philosophy*, 1847

To exercise power costs effort and demands courage. That is why so many fail to assert rights to which they are perfectly entitled— because a right is a kind of *power* but they are too lazy or too cowardly to exercise it. The virtues which cloak these faults are called *patience* and *forbearance*.
— FRIEDRICH NIETZSCHE (1844–1900), *The Wanderer and His Shadow*, 1880

To punish a man because he has committed a crime, or because he is believed, though unjustly, to have committed a crime, is not persecution. To punish a man, because we infer from the nature of some doctrine which he holds, or from the conduct of other persons who hold the same doctrines with him, that he will commit a crime, is persecution, and is, in every case, foolish and wicked.

— THOMAS BABINGTON MACAULAY (1800–1859), "Hallam's Constitutional History," 1828, reprinted in *Critical and Historical Essays,* 1843

Even today a crude sort of persecution is all that is required to create an *honorable* name for any sect, no matter how indifferent in itself.

— FRIEDRICH NIETZSCHE (1844–1900), *The Anti-Christ,* 1895

I am obliged to confess that I do not regard the abolition of slavery as a means of warding off the struggle of the two races in the Southern states. The Negroes may long remain slaves without complaining; but if they are once raised to the level of freemen, they will soon revolt at being deprived of almost all their civil rights; and as they cannot become the equals of the whites, they will speedily show themselves as enemies.

— ALEXIS DE TOCQUEVILLE (1805–1859), *Democracy in America,* 1840

Order

When we walk the streets at night in safety, it does not strike us that this might be otherwise. This habit of feeling safe has become second nature, and we do not reflect on just how this is due solely to the working of special institutions. Commonplace thinking often has the impression that force holds the state together, but in fact its only bond is the fundamental sense of order which everybody possesses.

— GEORG HEGEL (1770–1831), *The Philosophy of Right,* 1821

≋ *"Our" Times—and* ≋
the Times to Come

We are becoming like cats, slyly parasitic, enjoying an indifferent domesticity. Nice and snug in "the social," our historic passions have withdrawn into the glow of an artificial cosiness, and our half-closed eyes now seek little other than the peaceful parade of television pictures.

　　━ JEAN BAUDRILLARD (1929–　　), *Cool Memories,* 1987

This we take it is the grand characteristic of our age [the nineteenth century]. By our skill in Mechanism, it has come to pass, that in the management of external things we excel all other ages; while in whatever respects the pure moral nature, in true dignity of soul and character, we are perhaps inferior to most civilised ages.

　　━ THOMAS CARLYLE (1795–1881), *Signs of the Times,* 1829

We were wise indeed, could we discern truly the signs of our own time; and by knowledge of its wants and advantages, wisely adjust our own position in it. Let us, instead of gazing idly into the obscure distance, look calmly around us, for a little, on the perplexed scene where we stand. Perhaps, on a more serious inspection, something of its perplexity will disappear, some of its distinctive characters and deeper tendencies more clearly reveal themselves; whereby our own relations to it, our own true aims and endeavours in it, may also become clearer.

　　━ THOMAS CARLYLE (1795–1881), *Signs of the Times,* 1829

We stand today on the edge of a new frontier—the frontier of the 1960s, a frontier of unknown opportunities and perils, a frontier of unfulfilled hopes and threats. . . . The new frontier of which I speak is not a set of promises—it is a set of challenges.

　　━ JOHN F. KENNEDY (1917–1963), speech, July 13, 1960

The twentieth century was, without question, the most momentous . . . in the history of Mankind. It opened with the conquest of the air, and before it had run half its course had presented civilization with its supreme challenge—the control of atomic energy. Yet even these events were soon to be eclipsed. To us . . . the whole story of Mankind before the twentieth century seems like the prelude to some great drama, played on the narrow strip of stage before the curtain has risen and revealed the scenery. . . . Yet towards the close of that fabulous century, the curtain began slowly, inexorably, to rise. . . . The coming of the rocket brought to an end a million years of isolation. With the landing of the the first spaceships on Mars and Venus, the childhood of our race was over and history as we know it began. . . .

— ARTHUR C. CLARKE (1917–   ), *The Exploration of Space*, 1952

The Sage of Toronto [Marshall McLuhan] . . . spent several decades marveling at the numerous freedoms created by a "global village" instantly and effortlessly accessible to all. Villages, unlike towns, have always been ruled by conformism, isolation, petty surveillance, boredom and repetitive malicious gossip about the same families. Which is a precise enough description of the global spectacle's present vulgarity.

— GUY DEBORD (1931–   ), *Comments on the Society of the Spectacle*, 1988

It takes a kind of shabby arrogance to survive in our time, and a fairly romantic nature to want to.

— EDGAR Z. FRIEDENBERG (1921–   ), *The Vanishing Adolescent*, 1959

When you automate an industry, you modernize it; when you automate a life, you primitivize it.

— ERIC HOFFER (1902–1983), *Reflections on the Human Condition*, 1973

The trouble with our age is that it is all signpost and no destination.

— LOUIS KRONENBERGER (1904–1980), *Company Manners*, 1954

In societies where modern conditions of production prevail, all of life presents itself as an immense accumulation of *spectacles*. Everything that was directly lived has moved away into a representation.
— GUY DEBORD (1931–   ), *The Society of the Spectacle,* 1967

It is a tribute to the peculiar horror of contemporary life that it makes the worst features of earlier times—the stupefaction of the masses, the obsessed and driven lives of the bourgeoisie—seem attractive by comparison.
— CHRISTOPHER LASCH (1932–   ), *The Culture of Narcissism,* 1979

The sickness of our times for me has been just this damn thing that everything has been getting smaller and smaller and less and less important, that the romantic spirit has dried up, that there is no shame today. . . . We're all getting so mean and small and petty and ridiculous, and we all live under the threat of extermination.
— NORMAN MAILER (1923–   ), "Hip, Hell, and the Navigator," 1959, in *Advertisements for Myself,* 1959

The car has become the carapace, the protective and aggressive shell, of urban and suburban man.
— MARSHALL McLUHAN (1911–1980), *Understanding Media,* 1964

The mark of our time is its revulsion against imposed patterns.
— MARSHALL McLUHAN (1911–1980), *Understanding Media,* 1964

If the nineteenth century was the age of the editorial chair, ours is the century of the psychiatrist's couch.
— MARSHALL McLUHAN (1911–1980), *Understanding Media,* 1964

Yes. I think living right now is one of the most interesting of all times. If living back [in the nineteenth century] meant that I couldn't live now, I would definitely stay here. I would hate to have to face the kind of dentistry they had then.
— DAVID McCULLOUGH (1933–   ), interview with Roger Mudd, in *Great Minds of History,* 1999

There is one great fact, characteristic of this our nineteenth century, a fact which no party dares deny. On the one hand, there have started into life industrial and scientific forces which no epoch of former human history had ever suspected. On the other hand, there exist symptoms of decay, far surpassing the horrors recorded of the latter times of the Roman empire. In our days everything seems pregnant with its contrary.

➤ KARL MARX (1818–1883), speech, April 14, 1856

Unable to create a meaningful life for itself, the personality takes its own revenge: from the lower depths comes a regressive form of spontaneity: raw animality forms a counterpoise to the meaningless stimuli and the vicarious life to which the ordinary man is conditioned. Getting spiritual nourishment from this chaos of events, sensations, and devious interpretations is the equivalent of trying to pick through a garbage pile for food.

➤ LEWIS MUMFORD (1895–1990), *The Conduct of Life*, 1951

The clock, not the steam-engine, is the key machine of the modern industrial age.

➤ LEWIS MUMFORD (1895–1990), *Technics and Civilization*, 1934

The last man of the world-city no longer *wants* to live—he may cling to life as an individual, but as a type, as an aggregate, no, for it is a characteristic of this collective existence that it eliminates the terror of death.

➤ OSWALD SPENGLER (1880–1936), *The Decline of the West*, 1928

The fate of our times is characterized by rationalization and intellectualization and, above all, by the "disenchantment of the world." Precisely the ultimate and most sublime values have retreated from public life either into the transcendental realm of mystic life or into the brotherliness of direct and personal human relations. It is not accidental that our greatest art is intimate and not monumental.

➤ MAX WEBER (1864–1920), *Science as a Vocation*, 1917

Future biographers and historians are going to have an impossible time writing about us. We don't write letters. We don't keep diaries. They are going to think we talked like business memoranda, which is a great shame.

> ⬥ DAVID MCCULLOUGH (1933–   ), interview with Roger Mudd, in *Great Minds of History,* 1999

The Past

Many pundits today are in the habit of misquoting Santayana's epigram, "Those who cannot remember the past are condemned to repeat it." Maybe some people have come to grief this way, but they are probably fewer than those who have fallen into the opposite error. "One is apt to perish in politics from too much memory," Tocqueville wrote somewhere, with equal truth and greater insight.

> ⬥ DAVID HACKETT FISCHER (1935–   ), *Historians' Fallacies: Toward a Logic of Historical Thought,* 1970

Because men really respect only that which was founded of old and has developed slowly, he who wants to live on after his death must take care not only of his posterity but even more of his past.

> ⬥ FRIEDRICH NIETZSCHE (1844–1900), *Assorted Opinions and Maxims,* 1879

It is indeed a desirable thing to be well-descended, but the glory belongs to our ancestors.

> ⬥ PLUTARCH (before 50–after 120), "On the Training of Children"

The past is but the beginning of a beginning, and all that is and has been is but the twilight of the dawn.

> ⬥ H. G. WELLS (1866–1946), *The Discovery of the Future,* 1901

I don't think there are particular lessons to be learned from any particular event in the past. But what the past does teach you is wisdom—the sense of being part of a larger process. There are circumstances, cultural traditions, histories that impinge on you and prevent you from doing certain things. To be aware of those conditions, to be aware of those circumstances, is important for decision makers in the present.

— GORDON WOOD (1933–   ), interview with Roger Mudd, in *Great Minds of History,* 1999

 *Patriotism*

Patriotism is in political life what faith is in religion.

— LORD ACTON (1834–1902), "Nationality," 1862, in *Historical Essays and Studies,* 1907

Tribalism is the strongest force at work in the world today.

— VINE DELORIA, JR. (1933–   ), *Custer Died for Your Sins,* 1969

Historians are to nationalism what poppy-growers in Pakistan are to heroin addicts: we supply the essential raw material for the market.

— ERIC HOBSBAWM (1917–   ), lecture to the American Anthropological Association, published in *Anthropology Today,* 1992

It seems that American patriotism measures itself against an outcast group. The right Americans are the right Americans because they're not like the wrong Americans, who are not really Americans.

— ERIC HOBSBAWM (1917–   ), *Marxism Today,* 1988

While I am alive I shall never be in such slavery as to forgo my own kindred, or forget the laws of our forefathers.

— FLAVIUS JOSEPHUS (37–ca. 95), *The Wars of the Jews*

A man who is good enough to shed his blood for his country is good enough to be given a square deal afterwards. More than that no man is entitled to, and less than that no man shall have.

— THEODORE ROOSEVELT (1858–1919), speech, June 4, 1903

The first requisite of a good citizen in this republic of ours is that he shall be able and willing to pull his weight.

— THEODORE ROOSEVELT (1858–1919), speech, November 11, 1902

Philosophy

Philosophy: unintelligible answers to insoluble problems.

— HENRY BROOK ADAMS (1838–1918), in Leston Taylor,
The So-Called Human Race, 1922

Philosophy stands in the same relation to the study of the actual world as masturbation to sexual love.

— KARL MARX (1818–1883) and FRIEDRICH ENGELS (1820–1895),
The German Ideology, 1846

Actual philosophers . . . are commanders and law-givers: they say "thus it shall be!" It is they who determine the Wherefore and Whither of mankind, and they possess for this task the preliminary work of all the philosophical labourers, of all those who have subdued the past—they reach for the future with creative hand, and everything that is or has been becomes for them a means, an instrument, a hammer. Their "knowing" is *creating,* their creating is a law-giving, their will to truth is—*will to power.* Are there such philosophers today? Have there been such philosophers? *Must* there not be such philosophers?

— FRIEDRICH NIETZSCHE (1844–1900), *Beyond Good and Evil*, 1886

Truth in philosophy means that concept and external reality correspond.
— GEORG HEGEL (1770–1831), *The Philosophy of Right*, 1821

The philosophers have only *interpreted* the world in various ways; the point, however, is to *change* it.
— KARL MARX (1818–1883), *Theses on Feuerbach*, written 1845; published 1888

The philosopher believes that the value of his philosophy lies in the whole, in the building: posterity discovers it in the bricks with which he built and which are then often used again for better building: in the fact, that is to say, that that building can be destroyed and *nonetheless* possess value as material.
— FRIEDRICH NIETZSCHE (1844–1900), *Assorted Opinions and Maxims*, 1879

Bishop Berkeley destroyed this world in one volume octavo; and nothing remained, after his time, but mind; which experienced a similar fate from the hand of Mr. Hume in 1737.
— SYDNEY SMITH (1771–1845), *Sketches of Moral Philosophy*, 1850

Politics

Only he has the calling for politics who is sure that he will not crumble when the world from his point of view is too stupid or base for what he wants to offer. Only he who in the face of all this can say "In spite of all!" has the calling for politics.
— MAX WEBER (1864–1920), *Politics as a Vocation*, 1919

Politics is war by other means these days.
— ERIC ALTERMAN (1960–   ), radio interview, 1995

No man should be in politics unless he would honestly rather not be there.

— HENRY BROOK ADAMS (1838–1918), *The Education of Henry Adams,* 1907

Practical politics consists in ignoring facts.

— HENRY BROOK ADAMS (1838–1918), *The Education of Henry Adams,* 1907

[The politician:] Little other than a redtape Talking-machine, and unhappy Bag of Parliamentary Eloquence.

— THOMAS CARLYLE (1795–1881), *Latter-Day Pamphlets,* 1850

That most basic rule in politics: always stay in with the outs.

— DAVID HALBERSTAM (1934–   ), *The Best and the Brightest,* 1972

As in private life one differentiates between what a man thinks and says of himself and what he really is and does, so in historical struggles one must still more distinguish the language and the imaginary aspirations of parties from their real organism and their real interests, their conception of themselves from their reality.

— KARL MARX (1818–1883), *The Eighteenth Brumaire of Louis Bonaparte,* 1852

The Tories in England had long imagined that they were enthusiastic about the monarchy, the church and beauties of the old English Constitution, until the day of danger wrung from them the confession that they are enthusiastic only about rent.

— KARL MARX (1818–1883), *The Eighteenth Brumaire of Louis Bonaparte,* 1852

In the domain of Political Economy, free scientific inquiry meets not merely the same enemies as in all other domains. The peculiar nature of the material it deals with, summons as foes into the field of battle the most violent, mean and malignant passions of the human breast, the Furies of private interest.

— KARL MARX (1818–1883), *Capital,* 1867

The human being is in the most literal sense a political animal, not merely a gregarious animal, but an animal which can individuate itself only in the midst of society.

— KARL MARX (1818–1883), *Grundrisse,* 1858

Politics will eventually be replaced by imagery. The politician will be only too happy to abdicate in favor of his image, because the image will be much more powerful than he could ever be.

— MARSHALL MCLUHAN (1911–1980), in *Maclean's,* June 1971

The successor to politics will be propaganda. Propaganda, not in the sense of a message or ideology, but as the impact of the whole technology of the times.

— MARSHALL MCLUHAN (1911–1980), in *Maclean's,* June 1971

The newspaper reader says: this party will ruin itself if it makes errors like this. My *higher* politics says: a party which makes errors like this is already finished—it is no longer secure in its instincts.

— FRIEDRICH NIETZSCHE (1844–1900), *Twilight of the Idols,* 1889

There is nothing more agreeable in life than to make peace with the Establishment—and nothing more corrupting.

— A. J. P. TAYLOR (1906–1990), "William Cobbett," *New Statesman,* August 29, 1953

One can say that three preeminent qualities are decisive for the politician: passion, a feeling of responsibility, and a sense of proportion.

— MAX WEBER (1864–1920), *Politics as a Vocation,* 1919

The success of a party means little more than that the Nation is using the party for a large and definite purpose. . . . It seeks to use and interpret a change in its own plans and point of view.

— WOODROW WILSON (1856–1924), **first inaugural address,** 1913

We are apt to say that a foreign policy is successful only when the country, or at any rate the governing class, is united behind it. In reality, every line of policy is repudiated by a section, often by an influential section, of the country concerned. A foreign minister who waited until everyone agreed with him would have no foreign policy at all.

— A. J. P. TAYLOR (1906–1990), *The Trouble Makers*, 1957

 *Poverty*

Poverty in itself does not make men into a rabble; a rabble is created only when there is joined to poverty a disposition of mind, an inner indignation against the rich, against society, against the government.

— GEORG HEGEL (1770–1831), *The Philosophy of Right*, 1821

 *Power*

Power tends to corrupt and absolute power corrupts absolutely.

— LORD ACTON (1834–1902), letter to Bishop Mandell Creighton, April 5, 1887

He too serves a certain purpose who only stands and cheers.

— HENRY BROOK ADAMS (1838–1918), *The Education of Henry Adams*, 1907

A friend in power is a friend lost.

— HENRY BROOK ADAMS (1838–1918), *The Education of Henry Adams*, 1907

There is strength in the union even of very sorry men.

— HOMER (ca. 700 B.C.), *Iliad*

Power is poison. Its effect on Presidents had always been tragic.

— HENRY BROOK ADAMS (1838–1918), *The Education
of Henry Adams,* 1907

An appeaser is one who feeds a crocodile, hoping it will eat him last.

— WINSTON CHURCHILL (1874–1965), quoted in *The Reader's Digest,*
1954

In the eighteenth-century European balance of power, territory, population, and agriculture provided the basis for infantry, and France was a principal beneficiary. In the nineteenth century, industrial capacity provided the resources that enabled Britain, and later Germany, to gain dominance. By the mid-twentieth century, science and particularly nuclear physics contributed crucial power resources to the United States and the Soviet Union. In the next century, information technology, broadly defined, is likely to be the most important power resource.

— R. O. KEOHANE (1941–   ) and J. S. NYE, JR. (1937–   ),
"Power and Interdependence in the Information Age,"
Foreign Affairs, September/October 1998

The power elite is not so noticeable as the celebrities, and often does not want to be; the "power" of the professional celebrity is the power of distraction.

— C. WRIGHT MILLS (1916–1962), *The Power Elite,* 1956

Not necessity, not desire—no, the love of power is the demon of men. Let them have everything—health, food, a place to live, entertainment—they are and remain unhappy and low-spirited: for the demon waits and waits and will be satisfied.

— FRIEDRICH NIETZSCHE (1844–1900), *Daybreak,* 1881

I trust that a graduate student some day will write a doctoral essay on the influence of the Munich analogy on the subsequent history of the twentieth century. Perhaps in the end he will conclude that the multitude of errors committed in the name of "Munich" may exceed the original error of 1938.

— ARTHUR SCHLESINGER, JR. (1917–   ), *The Bitter Heritage:
Vietnam and American Democracy,* 1967

Press and Media

The press is the hired agent of a monied system, and set up for no other purpose than to tell lies where their interests are involved. One can trust nobody and nothing.
 — HENRY BROOK ADAMS (1838–1918), *The Letters of Henry Adams,* 1938

The traditional novel form continues to enlarge our experience in those very areas where the wide-angle lens and the Cinerama screen tend to narrow it.
 — DANIEL J. BOORSTIN (1914–   ), *The Image: A Guide to Pseudo-Events in America,* 1961

I think there ought to be a club in which preachers and journalists could come together and have the sentimentalism of the one matched with the cynicism of the other. That ought to bring them pretty close to the truth.
 — REINHOLD NIEBUHR (1892–1971), *Leaves from the Notebook of a Tamed Cynic,* 1930

The punditocracy is a tiny group of highly visible political pontificators who make their living offering "inside political opinions and forecasts" in the elite national media. And it is their debate, rather than any semblance of a democratic one, that determines the parameters of political discourse in the nation today.
 — ERIC ALTERMAN (1960–   ), *Sound and Fury: The Washington Punditocracy and the Collapse of American Politics,* 1992

The medium is the message. This is merely to say that the personal and social consequences of any medium—that is, of any extension of ourselves—result from the new scale that is introduced into our affairs by each extension of ourselves, or by any new technology.
 — MARSHALL McLUHAN (1911–1980), *Understanding Media,* 1964

We need not be theologians to see that we have shifted responsibility for making the world interesting from God to the newspaperman.
— DANIEL J. BOORSTIN (1914–   ), *The Image: A Guide to Pseudo-Events in America,* 1961

The press today is an army with carefully organized weapons, the journalists its officers, the readers its soldiers. But, as in every army, the soldier obeys blindly, and the war aims and operating plans change without his knowledge. The reader neither knows nor is supposed to know the purposes for which he is used and the role he is to play. There is no more appalling caricature of freedom of thought. Formerly no one was allowed to think freely; now it is permitted, but no one is capable of it any more. Now people want to think only what they are supposed to want to think, and this they consider freedom.
— OSWALD SPENGLER (1880–1936), *The Decline of the West,* 1926

[On seeing D. W. Griffiths's movie *Birth of a Nation:*] It is like writing history with lightning. And my only regret is that it is all so terribly true.
— WOODROW WILSON (1856–1924), spoken 1915, quoted in *Bartlett's Familiar Quotations*

 *Privacy*

The more the data banks record about each one of us, the less we exist.
— MARSHALL MCLUHAN (1911–1980), *Playboy,* March 1969

Today, the degradation of the inner life is symbolized by the fact that the only place sacred from interruption is the private toilet.
— LEWIS MUMFORD (1895–1990), *The Culture of Cities,* 1938

Progress

The movement from unity to multiplicity, between 1200 and 1900, was unbroken in sequence, and rapid in acceleration. Prolonged one generation longer, it would require a new social mind. . . . Thus far, since five or ten thousand years, the mind has successfully reacted, and nothing yet proved that it would fail to react—but it would need to jump.

— HENRY BROOK ADAMS (1838–1918), *The Education of Henry Adams*, 1907

The improved American highway system . . . isolated the American-in-transit. On his speedway . . . he had no contact with the towns which he bypassed. If he stopped for food or gas, he was served no local fare or local fuel, but had one of Howard Johnson's nationally branded ice cream flavors, and so many gallons of Exxon. This vast ocean of superhighways was nearly as free of culture as the sea traversed by the *Mayflower* Pilgrims.

— DANIEL J. BOORSTIN (1914–   ), Reith Lecture, 1975, published in *The Exploring Spirit: America and the World Experience*, 1976

Human development is a form of chronological unfairness, since late-comers are able to profit by the labors of their predecessors without paying the same price.

— ALEXANDER HERZEN (1812–1870), quoted by Isaiah Berlin in his introduction to Franco Venturi, *Roots of Revolution*, 1952

Westward the course of empire takes its way . . .

— GEORGE BERKELEY (1685–1753), *On the Prospect of Planting Arts and Learning in America*, 1752

For man is not the creature and product of Mechanism; but, in a far truer sense, its creator and producer.

— THOMAS CARLYLE (1795–1881), *Signs of the Times*, 1829

When we can drain the Ocean into mill-ponds, and bottle up the Force of Gravity, to be sold by retail, in gas jars; then may we hope to comprehend the infinitudes of man's soul under formulas of Profit and Loss; and rule over this too, as over a patent engine, by checks, and valves, and balances.

— THOMAS CARLYLE (1795–1881), *Signs of the Times,* 1829

The plow is one of the most ancient and most valuable of man's inventions; but long before he existed the land was in fact regularly plowed, and still continues to be thus plowed by earthworms. It may be doubted whether there are many other animals which have played so important a part in the history of the world, as have these lowly organized creatures.

— CHARLES DARWIN (1809–1882), *The Formation of Vegetable Mold Through the Action of Worms,* 1881

Mankind always sets itself only such tasks as it can solve; since, looking at the matter more closely, we will always find that the task itself arises only when the material conditions necessary for its solution already exist or are at least in the process of formation.

— KARL MARX (1818–1883), *A Contribution to the Critique of Political Economy,* 1859

Colonial system, public debts, heavy taxes, protection, commercial wars, etc., these offshoots of the period of manufacture swell to gigantic proportions during the period of infancy of large-scale industry. The birth of the latter is celebrated by a vast, Herod-like slaughter of the innocents.

— KARL MARX (1818–1883), *Capital,* 1867

I firmly believe that before many centuries more, science will be master of man. The engine he will have invented will be beyond his strength to control. Some day science may have the existence of mankind in its power, and the human race commit suicide by blowing up the world.

— HENRY BROOK ADAMS (1838–1918), letter to his brother, George, April 11, 1862

The development of civilization and industry in general has always shown itself so active in the destruction of forests that everything that has been done for their conservation and production is completely insignificant in comparison.

— KARL MARX (1818–1883), *Capital*, 1867

We are becoming servants in thought, as in action, of the machines we have created to serve us.

— JOHN KENNETH GALBRAITH (1908–   ), *The New Industrial State*, 1967

The country that is more developed industrially only shows, to the less developed, the image of its own future.

— KARL MARX (1818–1883), *Capital*, 1867

Time advances: facts accumulate; doubts arise. Faint glimpses of truth begin to appear, and shine more and more unto the perfect day. The highest intellects, like the tops of mountains, are the first to catch and to reflect the dawn. They are bright, while the level below is still in darkness. But soon the light, which at first illuminated only the loftiest eminences, descends on the plain, and penetrates to the deepest valley. First come hints, then fragments of systems, then defective systems, then complete and harmonious systems. The sound opinion, held for a time by one bold speculator, becomes the opinion of a small minority, of a strong minority, of a majority of mankind. Thus, the great progress goes on.

— THOMAS BABINGTON MACAULAY (1800–1859), "History of the Revolution in England," 1835, in *Critical and Historical Essays Contributed to the Edinburgh Review*, 1843

Persons grouped around a fire or candle for warmth or light are less able to pursue independent thoughts, or even tasks, than people supplied with electric light. In the same way, the social and educational patterns latent in automation are those of self-employment and artistic autonomy.

— MARSHALL MCLUHAN (1911–1980), *Understanding Media*, 1964

We have created an industrial order geared to automatism, where feeble-mindedness, native or acquired, is necessary for docile productivity in the factory; and where a pervasive neurosis is the final gift of the meaningless life that issues forth at the other end.
  — LEWIS MUMFORD (1895–1990), *The Conduct of Life*, 1951

The vast material displacements the machine has made in our physical environment are perhaps in the long run less important than its spiritual contributions to our culture.
  — LEWIS MUMFORD (1895–1990), "The Drama of the Machines," *Scribner's*, August 1930

Today, the notion of progress in a single line without goal or limit seems perhaps the most parochial notion of a very parochial century.
  — LEWIS MUMFORD (1895–1990), *Technics and Civilization*, 1934

By his very success in inventing labor-saving devices, modern man has manufactured an abyss of boredom that only the privileged classes in earlier civilizations have ever fathomed.
  — LEWIS MUMFORD (1895–1990), *The Conduct of Life*, 1951

However far modern science and technics have fallen short of their inherent possibilities, they have taught mankind at least one lesson: Nothing is impossible.
  — LEWIS MUMFORD (1895–1990), *Technics and Civilization*, 1934

What has misled judgment in our own age is that the greatest technological achievements of the ancient world were in the realm of statics, not dynamics, in civil, not mechanical engineering: in buildings, not machines. If the historian finds a lack of invention in earlier cultures, it is because he persists in taking as the main criterion of mechanical progress the special kinds of power-driven machine or automation to which western man has now committed himself, while treating as negligible important inventions, like central heating and flush toilets—or even ignorantly attributing the latter to our own "industrial revolution."
  — LEWIS MUMFORD (1895–1990), *The Myth of the Machine*, 1967

The cycle of the machine is now coming to an end. Man has learned much in the hard discipline and the shrewd, unflinching grasp of practical possibilities that the machine has provided in the last three centuries: but we can no more continue to live in the world of the machine than we could live successfully on the barren surface of the moon.
— LEWIS MUMFORD (1895–1990), *The Culture of Cities*, 1938

Oh, how much is today hidden by science! Oh, how much it is expected to hide!
— FRIEDRICH NIETZSCHE (1844–1900), *The Genealogy of Morals*, 1887

Technologies always have unintended consequences, of course: Just think how the invention of type finally altered religious belief in northern Europe, or how artillery changed the shape of medieval cities, or how steam power opened up the American West. But mass production vastly accelerates and enlarges those consequences; it is the *scale* of technology's impact on human life that sets the Age of Mass Production apart.
— WITOLD RYBCZYNSKI (1943–   ), "The Ceaseless Machine: The Coming of Mass Production," in Lorraine Glennon, ed., *Our Times: The Illustrated History of the 20th Century*, 1995

It is the Late city that first defies the land, contradicts Nature in the lines of its silhouette, *denies* all Nature. It wants to be something different from and higher than Nature. These high-pitched gables, these Baroque cupolas, spires, and pinnacles, neither are, nor desire to be, related with anything in Nature. And then begins the gigantic megalopolis, the *city-as-world,* which suffers nothing beside itself and sets about *annihilating* the country picture.
— OSWALD SPENGLER (1880–1936), *The Decline of the West*, 1926

The press, the machine, the railway, the telegraph are premises whose thousand-year conclusion no one has yet dared to draw.
— FRIEDRICH NIETZSCHE (1844–1900), *The Wanderer and His Shadow*, 1880

We believe that the most basic of all changes in human social organization have been the result of three processes. Starting 8000 to 10,000 years ago, agriculture was invented in the Middle East—probably by a woman. That's the First Wave. Roughly 250 years ago, the Industrial Revolution triggered a Second Wave of change. Brute-force technologies amplified human and animal muscle power and gave rise to an urban, factory-centered way of life. Sometime after World War II, a gigantic Third Wave began transforming the planet, based on tools that amplify mind rather than muscle. The Third Wave is bigger, deeper and faster than the other two. This is the civilization of the computer, the satellite and Internet.

— ALVIN TOFFLER (1928–   ), interview, *The New York Times*, June 11, 1995

But the nature of our civilized minds is so detached from the senses, even in the vulgar, by abstractions corresponding to all the abstract terms our languages abound in, and so refined by the art of writing, and as it were spiritualized by the use of numbers, because even the vulgar know how to count and reckon, that it is naturally beyond our power to form the vast image of this mistress called "Sympathetic Nature."

— GIAMBATTISTA VICO (1688–1744), *The New Science*, 1744

A radical is one of whom people say, "He goes too far." A conservative, on the other hand, is one who "doesn't go far enough." Then there is the reactionary, "one who doesn't go at all." All these terms are more or less objectionable, wherefore we have coined the term "progressive." I should say that a progressive is one who insists upon recognizing new facts as they present themselves—one who adjusts legislation to these new facts.

— WOODROW WILSON (1856–1924), *speech*, January 29, 1911

The thinking man, and what is still rarer, the man of taste, numbers only four ages in the history of the world; four happy ages when the arts were brought to perfection and which, marking an era of the greatness of the human mind, are an example to posterity.

The first of these ages, to which true glory belongs, is that of Philip and Alexander, or rather of Pericles, Demosthenes, Aristotle, Plato, Apelles, Phidias, Praxiteles; and this honour was confined within the limits of Greece, the rest of the known world being in a barbarous state.

The second age is that of Caesar and Augustus, distinguished moreover by the names of Lucretius, Cicero, Livy, Virgil, Horace, Ovid, Varro, and Vitruvius.

The third is that which followed the taking of Constantinople by Mohomet II . . . the hour of Italy's glory. . . .

The fourth age is that which we call the age of Louis XIV, and it is perhaps of the four the one which most nearly approaches perfection.

— VOLTAIRE (1694–1778), *The Age of Louis XIV*, 1751

Long ago the country bore the country-town and nourished it with her best blood. Now the giant city sucks the country dry, insatiably and incessantly demanding and devouring fresh streams of men, till it wearies and dies in the midst of an almost uninhabited waste of country.

— OSWALD SPENGLER (1880–1936), *The Decline of the West*, 1926

 *Public Opinion*

You may talk of the tyranny of Nero and Tiberius; but the real tyranny is the tyranny of your next-door neighbor. . . . Public opinion is a permeating influence, and it exacts obedience to itself, it requires us to think other men's thoughts, to speak other men's words, to follow other men's habits.

— WALTER BAGEHOT (1826–1877), *Biographical Studies*, 1907

Wonderful "Force of Public Opinion!" We must act and walk in all points as it prescribes; follow the traffic it bids us, realise the sum of money, the degree of "influence" it expects of us, or we shall be lightly esteemed; certain mouthfuls of articulate wind will be blown at us, and this what mortal courage can front?

— THOMAS CARLYLE (1795–1881), *Signs of the Times*, 1829

Public opinion contains all kinds of falsity and truth, but it takes a great man to find the truth in it. The great man of the age is the one who can put into words the will of his age, tell his age what its will is, and accomplish it. What he does is the heart and the essence of his age, he actualizes his age. The man who lacks sense enough to despise public opinion expressed in gossip will never do anything great.

— GEORG HEGEL (1770–1831), *The Philosophy of Right*, 1821

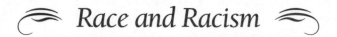

Race and Racism

The discrediting of racism may, paradoxically, prove to be Hitler's most enduring accomplishment. But some people have reacted in a mistaken way to the terrible crimes and atrocities which were committed in the name of race. They have tended to repudiate the idea of all hereditary characteristics, and to dismiss race as a dangerous superstition. Some racist thought is dangerous, but genetics remains a science. Race itself, properly understood, is a reality—a historical reality—at the same time that racism is a profound and bloody error, which cannot be tolerated in the contemporary world.

— DAVID HACKETT FISCHER (1935–   ), *Historians' Fallacies: Toward a Logic of Historical Thought*, 1970

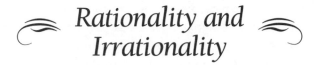 Rationality and Irrationality

Rational, that is to say, conforms to the necessity of things.
— ISAIAH BERLIN (1909–1997), *Two Concepts of Liberty,* 1958

To him who looks upon the world rationally, the world in its turn presents a rational aspect. The relation is mutual.
— GEORG HEGEL (1770–1831), *The Philosophy of History,* 1837

Keep to moderation, keep the end in view, follow nature.
— LUCAN (39–65), *The Civil War*

In the consciousness of the truth he has perceived, man now sees everywhere only the awfulness or the absurdity of existence . . . and loathing seizes him.
— FRIEDRICH NIETZSCHE (1844–1900), *The Birth of Tragedy,* 1872

The irrationality of a thing is no argument against its existence, rather a condition of it.
— FRIEDRICH NIETZSCHE (1844–1900), *Human, All Too Human,* 1878

 Reform

To reform a world, to reform a nation, no wise man will undertake; and all but foolish men know, that the only solid, though a far slower reformation, is what each begins and perfects on *himself.*
— THOMAS CARLYLE (1795–1881), *Signs of the Times,* 1829

The American tradition had been one of unusually widespread participation of the citizen in the management of affairs, both political and economic. Now the growth of the large corporation, the labor union, and the big impenetrable political machine was clotting society into large aggregates and presenting to the unorganized citizen the prospect that all these aggregates and interests would be able to act in concert and shut out those men for whom organization was difficult or impossible. . . . The central theme of Progressivism was this revolt against the industrial discipline: the Progressive movement was the complaint of the unorganized against the consequences of organization.

➤ RICHARD HOFSTADTER (1916–1970), *The Age of Reform*, 1955

Turn where we may, within, around, the voice of great events is proclaiming to us, Reform, that you may preserve!

➤ THOMAS BABINGTON MACAULAY (1800–1859), **Parliamentary speech supporting the Reform Bill, March 2, 1831**

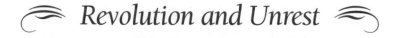

Revolution and Unrest

The short lesson that comes out of long experience in political agitation is something like this: *all* the motive power in all of these movements is the instinct of religious feeling. All the obstruction comes from attempting to rely on anything else. Conciliation is the enemy.

➤ JOHN JAY CHAPMAN (1862–1933), *Practical Agitation*, 1898

Like other revolutionaries I can thank God for the reactionaries. They clarify the issue.

➤ R. G. COLLINGWOOD (1889–1943), *An Autobiography*, 1939

All successful revolutions are the kicking in of a rotten door.

➤ JOHN KENNETH GALBRAITH (1908–   ), *The Age of Uncertainty*, 1977

The spirit of revolution, the spirit of insurrection, is a spirit radically opposed to liberty.

—FRANCOIS GUIZOT (1787–1874), speech, December 29, 1830

[On the failure of the European revolutions of 1848:] We have wasted our spirit in the regions of the abstract and general just as the monks let it wither in the world of prayer and contemplation.

—ALEXANDER HERZEN (1812–1870), *From the Other Shore*, 1849

[On the failure of the European revolutions of 1848:] No one is to blame. It is neither their fault nor ours. It is the misfortune of being born when a whole world is dying.

—ALEXANDER HERZEN (1812–1870), *From the Other Shore*, 1849

In revolutionary times the rich are always the people who are most afraid.

—GERALD WHITE JOHNSON (1890–1980), *American Freedom and the Press*, 1958

Revolutions are the locomotives of history.

—KARL MARX (1818–1883), quoted in Vladimir I. Lenin, *Two Tactics of Social Democracy in the Democratic Revolution*, 1905

[The Bolshevik Revolution:] Ten Days That Shook the World

—JOHN REED (1887–1920), *Ten Days That Shook the World*, 1919

Our worst revolutionaries today are those reactionaries who do not see and will not admit that there is any need for change.

—THEODORE ROOSEVELT (1858–1919), *Autobiography*, 1913

America is a young country with an old mentality. If there ever are great revolutions there, they will be caused by the presence of the blacks upon American soil. That is to say, it will not be the equality of social conditions but rather their inequality which may give rise to it.

—ALEXIS DE TOCQUEVILLE (1805–1859), *Democracy in America*, 1840

In every revolution there intrude, at the side of its true agents, men of a different stamp; some of them survivors of and devotees to past revolutions, without insight into the present movement, but preserving popular influence by their known honesty and courage, or by the sheer force of tradition; others mere brawlers, who, by dint of repeating year after year the same set of stereotyped declamations against the government of the day, have sneaked into the reputation of revolutionists of the first water. . . . They are an unavoidable evil: with time they are shaken off.

— KARL MARX (1818–1883), Address to the General Council of the International Working Men's Association on "The Civil War in France," 1871

It is almost never when a state of things is the most detestable that it is smashed, but when, beginning to improve, it permits men to breathe, to reflect, to communicate their thoughts with each other, and to gauge by what they already have the extent of their rights and their grievances. The weight, although less heavy, seems then all the more unbearable.

— ALEXIS DE TOCQUEVILLE (1805–1859), letter, September 23, 1853

Russia

Russia . . . is a riddle wrapped in a mystery inside an enigma.

— WINSTON CHURCHILL (1874–1965), radio broadcast, October 1, 1939

It is the Russians' joy to drink; we cannot do without it.

— THE PRIMARY CHRONICLE (early Russian historical work), 1040–1118

⌒ *Sense and Nonsense* ⌒

There are . . . insidious analogies in the verbs, adjectives, adverbs, and prepositions that historians conventionally use. Revolutions tend to "break out," as if they were dangerous maniacs, locked in a prison cell. Governments are overturned, like applecarts. Economies boom and bust, like a cowboy on a Saturday spree. Cultures flower and fade like a garden of forget-me-nots. Jefferson and Hamilton, or Pitt and Fox, tend to "thrust and parry" through the history books, like pairs of gentlemanly duelists. But Kennedy and Khrushchev, or Churchill and Hitler, bash and bludgeon like Friar Tuck and Little John.

— DAVID HACKETT FISCHER (1935–   ), *Historians' Fallacies: Toward a Logic of Historical Thought,* 1970

Robert Garland, the promoter of daylight-saving time, seriously suggested that boys who lived in daylight time zones had bigger feet than boys in other areas, and moreover that "bigger feet make better men." He concluded therefore that daylight time caused better men.

— DAVID HACKETT FISCHER (1935–   ), *Historians' Fallacies: Toward a Logic of Historical Thought,* 1970

The *reductive fallacy* reduces complexity to simplicity, or diversity to uniformity, in causal explanations. . . . For the want of a nail the shoe was lost, for the want of a shoe the horse was lost, for the want of a horse the rider was lost, for the want of a rider the message was lost, for the want of a message the regiment was lost, and for the want of a regiment the battle was lost. This exemplary anecdote has probably been told to every quartermaster in the Western world—no doubt with a salutary effect upon the supply of military horseshoe nails. I am told that our army still possesses a considerable quantity of them. But it has not helped our sense of history.

— DAVID HACKETT FISCHER (1935–   ), *Historians' Fallacies: Toward a Logic of Historical Thought,* 1970

The concept of cause being under a cloud (because it used to be employed too crudely) historians have for a time been hunting for a substitute. Wherever one turns in history today, one runs head-on into factors. There are no longer any causes of the Reformation; instead there are factors that made it possible. This is to go from tolerably dubious to the quite abominable. A cause is something real: people do things in order to get results. A factor—outside mathematics, and trading stations and Scottish estates—is a meaningless piece of tired jargon. Events are not the product of simple causes but of complex situations in which a variety of people and circumstances participates, but this does not mean that they are produced by factors. A word to be forgotten.

    — G. R. ELTON (1921–1994), *The Practice of History,* 1967

Many bad ideas have had a long life because of a good (effective) analogy. If analogy is used to persuade without proof, or to indoctrinate without understanding, or to settle an empirical question without empirical evidence, then it is misused. Sometimes the results are not merely disagreeable but downright dangerous. In the formation of postnuclear public policy, nothing is quite as lethal as a faulty prenuclear analogy.

    — DAVID HACKETT FISCHER (1935–   ), *Historians' Fallacies: Toward a Logic of Historical Thought,* 1970

Tended, grew out of, developed, evolved, trend, development, tendency, evolution, growth. Such words are like the sealed junction boxes on the complex circuits of history. One knows that inside the boxes there are connections which induce the currents of history to change direction; but the boxes conceal rather than reveal how those connections are made.

    — J. H. HEXTER (1910–1996), *Reappraisals in History,* 1961

Men are not machines. . . . They are men—a tautology which is sometimes worth remembering.

    — GILBERT RYLE (1900–1976), quoted in David Hackett Fischer, *Historians' Fallacies: Toward a Logic of Historical Thought,* 1970

The *pathetic fallacy* is the ascription of animate behavior to inanimate objects. . . . Most commonly, the pathetic fallacy takes the form of anthropomorphism and anthropathism, in which human form and human feelings are given to gods, groups, objects, etc. There are many examples of the pathetic fallacy in explicitly historical writing—by conservatives who fear the beast of Bolshevism, liberals who complain of the cunning of capitalism, intellectual historians who speak of the mind of the Enlightenment, and institutional historians who would have a bare-breasted Madame Liberty hitch up her skirts and hurdle the barricades, as in Delacroix's famous version of the Revolution of 1830.

— DAVID HACKETT FISCHER (1935–   ), *Historians' Fallacies: Toward a Logic of Historical Thought,* 1970

Common sense is judgment without reflection, shared by an entire class, an entire nation, or the entire human race.

— GIAMBATTISTA VICO (1688–1744), *The New Science,* 1744

The universal principle of etymology in all languages: words are carried over from bodies and from the properties of bodies to express the things of the mind and spirit. The order of ideas must follow the order of things.

— GIAMBATTISTA VICO (1688–1744), *The New Science,* 1744

 *Sport*

Sport in the sense of a mass-spectacle, with death to add to the underlying excitement, comes into existence when a population has been drilled and regimented and depressed to such an extent that it needs at least a vicarious participation in difficult feats of strength or skill or heroism in order to sustain its waning life-sense.

— LEWIS MUMFORD (1895–1990), *Technics and Civilization,* 1934

Whoever wants to know the heart and mind of America had better learn baseball, the rules and realities of the game—and do it by watching first some high school or small-town teams.

— JACQUES BARZUN (1907–   ), *God's Country and Mine*, 1954

"The battle of Waterloo was won on the playing fields of Eton."

— SIR WILLIAM FRASER (1826–1898), quotation attributed to the Duke of Wellington, in *Words on Wellington*, 1889

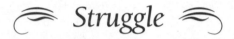

Struggle

We combat obstacles in order to get repose, and, when got, the repose is insupportable.

— HENRY BROOK ADAMS (1838–1918), *The Education of Henry Adams*, 1907

But it pleased God to visit us then with death daily, and with so general a disease that the living were scarce able to bury the dead.

— WILLIAM BRADFORD (1590–1657), *Of Plimoth Plantation*, 1647

Never give in, never give in, never, never, never, never—in nothing, great or small, large or petty—never give in except to conviction of honor and good sense.

— WINSTON CHURCHILL (1874–1965), speech at Harrow School, October 29, 1941

As regards the celebrated "struggle for *life*," it seems to me for the present to have been rather asserted than proved. It does occur, but as the exception; the general aspect of life is *not* hunger and distress, but rather wealth, luxury, even absurd prodigality—where there is a struggle it is a struggle for *power*.

— FRIEDRICH NIETZSCHE (1844–1900), *Twilight of the Idols*, 1889

Adversity is sometimes hard upon a man; but for one man who can stand prosperity, there are a hundred that will stand adversity.
— THOMAS CARLYLE (1795–1881), *On Heroes, Hero-Worship, and the Heroic in History,* 1841

Every new baby is a blind desperate vote for survival: people who find themselves unable to register an effective political protest against extermination do so by a biological act.
— LEWIS MUMFORD (1895–1990), *The City in History,* 1961

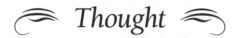

Thought

To most people nothing is more troublesome than the effort of thinking.
— JAMES BRYCE (1838–1922), *Studies in History and Jurisprudence,* 1901

Thought once awakened does not again slumber; unfolds itself into a System of Thought; grows, in man after man, generation after generation, till its full stature is reached, and *such* System of Thought can grow no farther, but must give place to another.
— THOMAS CARLYLE (1795–1881), *On Heroes, Hero-Worship, and the Heroic in History,* 1841

Physical concepts are free creations of the human mind, and are not, however it may seem, uniquely determined by the external world.
— ALBERT EINSTEIN (1879–1955), *Evolution of Physics,* 1938

An idea is always a generalization, and generalization is a property of thinking. To generalize means to think.
— GEORG HEGEL (1770–1831), *The Philosophy of Right,* 1821

For tribal man space was the uncontrollable mystery. For techno-logical man it is time that occupies the same role.
— MARSHALL MCLUHAN (1911–1980), *The Mechanical Bride*, 1951

Thoughts are the shadows of our sensations—always darker, emp-tier, simpler than these.
— FRIEDRICH NIETZSCHE (1844–1900), *The Gay Science*, 1887

Truth and Perception

No historian really treats all facts as unique; he treats them as par-ticular. He cannot—no one can—deal in unique fact, because facts and events require reference to common experience, to conven-tional frameworks, to (in short) the general before they acquire meaning. The unique event of a freak and a frustration; if it is really unique—can never recur in meaning or implication—it lacks every measurable dimension and cannot be assessed. But to the histo-rian, facts and events (and people) must be individual and particu-lar: *like* other entities of a similar kind, but never entirely identical with them. That is to say, they are to be treated as peculiar to them-selves and not as indistinguishable statistical units or elements in an equation; but they are linked and rendered comprehensible by kinship, by common possessions, by universal qualities present in differing proportions and arrangements.
— G. R. ELTON (1921–1994), *The Practice of History*, 1967

The song of the barnyard cock is *cock-a-doodle-do* in English, *cocorico* in French, and *kikiericki* in German and in Italian. Would anyone debate on which is right or whether cocks in different countries sing different songs?
— GEORGE BOAS, quoted in David Hackett Fischer, *Historians' Fallacies: Toward a Logic of Historical Thought*, 1970

Ideology has very little to do with "consciousness." . . . It is profoundly *unconscious*.
— Louis Althusser (1918–), *For Marx*, 1965

One of the first duties of man is not to be duped.
— Carl Becker (1873–1945), quoted in David Hackett Fischer,
Historians' Fallacies: Toward a Logic of Historical Thought, 1970

The prevailing opinion in the trenches [of World War I] was that anything might be true, except what was printed.
— Marc Bloch, *The Historian's Craft*, 1953

Men willingly believe what they wish.
— Julius Caesar (100–44 B.C.), *The Gallic War*

I grow daily to honour facts more and more, and theory less and less. A fact, it seems to me, is a great thing—a sentence printed, if not by God, then at least by the Devil.
— Thomas Carlyle (1795–1881), letter, April 29, 1836

The impossible object is a quest for the whole truth—a quest which characteristically takes one of three forms. Occasionally, it consists in an attempt to know everything about everything. Sometimes it seeks to learn something about everything. Most often it is a search for everything about something. None of these purposes is remotely realizable. A historian can only hope to know something about something.
— David Hackett Fischer (1935–), *Historians' Fallacies:
Toward a Logic of Historical Thought*, 1970

In the beautiful, man sets himself up as the standard of perfection; in select cases he worships himself in it. . . . Man believes that the world itself is filled with beauty—he *forgets* that it is he who has created it. He alone has bestowed beauty upon the world—alas! only a very human, an all too human, beauty.
— Friedrich Nietzsche (1844–1900), *Twilight of the Idols*, 1889

It is no easy matter to tell the truth, pure and simple, about past events; for historical truths are never pure, and rarely simple.
— DAVID HACKETT FISCHER (1935–   ), *Historians' Fallacies: Toward a Logic of Historical Thought*, 1970

A good many scholars would prefer not to know that some things exist. But not knowing that a thing exists is different from knowing that it does not exist. The former is never sound proof of the latter. Not to know that something exists is to imply not knowing. One thinks of Alice and the White Knight:

> "I see nobody on the road," said Alice.
> "I only wish *I* had such eyes," the Knight
> remarked in a fretful tone. "To be able to
> see Nobody! And at that distance too!"

— DAVID HACKETT FISCHER (1935–   ), *Historians' Fallacies: Toward a Logic of Historical Thought*, 1970

A historian who swears to tell nothing but the whole truth, would thereby take a vow of eternal silence.
— DAVID HACKETT FISCHER (1935–   ), *Historians' Fallacies: Toward a Logic of Historical Thought*, 1970

As a humanist, I am bound to reply that almost all important questions are important precisely because they are not susceptible to quantitative answers.
— ARTHUR SCHLESINGER, JR. (1917–   ), "The Humanist Looks at Empirical Social Research," *American Sociological Review*, 27, 1962

Truth, naked, unblushing truth, the first virtue of all serious history, must be the sole recommendation of this personal narrative.
— EDWARD GIBBON (1737–1794), *Memoirs of My Life*, 1796

The laws of probability, so true in general, so fallacious in particular.
— EDWARD GIBBON (1737–1794), *Memoirs*, 1796

Men trust their ears less than their eyes.
— HERODOTUS (ca. 484–after 424 B.C.), *The Histories of Herodotus*

Generalisation is necessary to the advancement of knowledge; but particularly is indispensable to the creations of the imagination. In proportion as men know more and think more they look less at individuals and more at classes. They therefore make better theories and worse poems.

— THOMAS BABINGTON MACAULAY (1800–1859), "Milton," 1825, reprinted in *Critical and Historical Essays*, 1843

What then in the last resort are the truths of mankind?— They are the *irrefutable* errors of mankind.

— FRIEDRICH NIETZSCHE (1844–1900), *The Gay Science*, 1887

We operate with nothing but things which do not exist, with lines, planes, bodies, atoms, divisible time, divisible space—how should explanation even be possible when we first make everything into an *image,* into our own image!

— FRIEDRICH NIETZSCHE (1844–1900), *The Gay Science*, 1887

Not when truth is dirty, but when it is shallow, does the enlightened man dislike to wade into its waters.

— FRIEDRICH NIETZSCHE (1844–1900), *Thus Spoke Zarathustra*, 1884

Our belief in any particular natural law cannot have a safer basis than our unsuccessful critical attempts to refute it.

— KARL POPPER (1902–1994), *Conjectures and Refutations*, 1963

Uniform ideas originating among entire peoples unknown to each other must have a common ground of truth.

— GIAMBATTISTA VICO (1688–1744), *The New Science*, 1744

In the case of news, we should always wait for the sacrament of confirmation.

— VOLTAIRE (1694–1778), letter, August 28, 1760

To the living we owe respect, but to the dead we owe only the truth.

— VOLTAIRE (1694–1778), "First Letter on Oedipus," 1719, in *The Portable Voltaire*, 1968

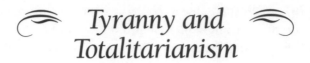

Tyranny and Totalitarianism

Dictators ride to and from upon tigers which they dare not dismount. And the tigers are getting hungry.

— Winston Churchill (1874–1965), *While England Slept,* 1936

It seems to be in the nature of imperialism to fear everything that is not subject to its influence.

— Mansour Farhang (1936–   ), *U.S. Imperialism: The Spanish-American War to the Iranian Revolution,* 1981

The urgent consideration of the public safety may undoubtedly authorise the violation of every positive law. How far that or any other consideration may operate to dissolve the natural obligations of humanity and justice, is a doctrine of which I still desire to remain ignorant.

— Edward Gibbon (1737–1794), *The Decline and Fall of the Roman Empire,* 1776–1788

Many politicians of our time are in the habit of laying it down as a self-evident proposition that no people ought to be free till they are fit to use their freedom. The maxim is worthy of the fool in the old story who resolved not to go into the water until he had learnt to swim. If men are to wait for liberty till they become wise and good in slavery, they may indeed wait forever.

— Thomas Babington Macaulay (1800–1859), "Milton," 1825, reprinted in *Critical and Historical Essays,* 1843

Since it is difficult to join them together, it is safer to be feared than to be loved when one of the two must be lacking.

— Niccolò Machiavelli (1469–1527), *The Prince,* 1514

The reluctant obedience of distant provinces generally costs more than it [the territory] is worth. Empires which branch out widely are often more flourishing for a little timely pruning.
— THOMAS BABINGTON MACAULAY (1800–1859), "War of the Succession in Spain," 1833, reprinted in *Critical and Historical Essays,* 1843

Perhaps the totalitarian impulse, the craving for absolute order in times of frightening chaos, transcends the philosophical differences—over who should own the means of production, over whether nation or class is paramount—that once made fascism and communism seem so fundamentally opposed. No immunization against political chaos has yet been found, and so nations return again and again to a drastic, and terribly destructive, cure.
— STEPHEN SPENDER (1909–1995), "Nations in Goose Step: The Age of Totalitarianism," in Lorraine Glennon, ed., *Our Times: The Illustrated History of the 20th Century,* 1995

Urban Life

The chief function of the city is to convert power into form, energy into culture, dead matter into the living symbols of art, biological reproduction into social creativity.
— LEWIS MUMFORD (1895–1990), *The City in History,* 1961

The city is a fact in nature, like a cave, a run of mackerel or an antheap. But it is also a conscious work of art, and it holds within its communal framework many simpler and more personal forms of art. Mind *takes form* in the city, and in turn, urban forms condition mind.
— LEWIS MUMFORD (1895–1990), *The Culture of Cities,* 1938

In place of a world, there is a *city,* a *point,* in which the whole life of broad regions is collecting while the rest dries up. In place of a type-true people, born of and grown on the soil, there is a new sort of nomad, cohering unstably in fluid masses, the parasitical city dweller, traditionless, utterly matter-of-fact, religionless, clever, unfruitful, deeply contemptuous of the countryman and especially that highest form of countryman, the country gentleman.

—OSWALD SPENGLER (1880–1936), *The Decline of the West,* 1926

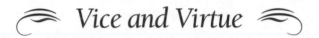 *Vice and Virtue*

I do not find fault with equality for drawing men into the pursuit of forbidden pleasures, but for absorbing them entirely in the search for the pleasures that are permitted.

—ALEXIS DE TOCQUEVILLE (1805–1859), *Democracy in America,* 1840

Mere goodness can achieve little against the power of nature.

—GEORG HEGEL (1770–1831), *The Philosophy of Right,* 1821

Vice may be had in abundance with trouble; the way is smooth and her dwelling place is near. But before virtue the gods have set toil.

—HESIOD (8th century B.C.), quoted in Plato, *The Republic*

The fact is that a man who wants to act virtuously in every way necessarily comes to grief among so many who are not virtuous.

—NICCOLÒ MACHIAVELLI (1469–1527), *The Prince,* 1514

All good things were at one time bad things; every original sin has developed into an original virtue.

—FRIEDRICH NIETZSCHE (1844–1900), *The Genealogy of Morals,* 1887

A prince must be prudent enough to know how to escape the bad reputation of those vices that would lose the state for him, and must protect himself from those that will not lose it for him, if this is possible; but if he cannot, he need not concern himself unduly if he ignores these less serious vices.

— NICCOLÒ MACHIAVELLI (1469–1527), *The Prince*, 1514

We do not place especial value on the possession of a virtue until we notice its total absence in our opponent.

— FRIEDRICH NIETZSCHE (1844–1900), *Human, All Too Human*, 1878

Men first feel necessity, then look for utility, next attend to comfort, still later amuse themselves with pleasure, thence grow dissolute in luxury, and finally go mad and waste their substance.

— GIAMBATTISTA VICO (1688–1744), *The New Science*, 1744

Time, which alone makes the reputation of men, ends by making their defects respectable.

— VOLTAIRE (1694–1778), *Letters on England*, 1732

 *War*

War with Mexico followed America's expansionist spree as inevitably as night follows day. The annexation of Texas and President Polk's blatant demands for California left a legacy of hatred that the best will in the world could not have resolved—and that will was lacking.

— RAY ALLEN BILLINGTON (1903–1981), *The Far Western Frontier: 1830–1860*, 1956

In war there is no second prize for the runner-up.

— OMAR BRADLEY (1893–1981), *Military Review*, 1950

By 1970, more bombs had been dropped on Vietnam than all targets in the whole of human history.

> — STEPHEN AMBROSE, (1936–   ), *Rise to Globalism: American Foreign Policy, 1938–1980,* 1980

The first accounts we have of mankind are but accounts of their butcheries. All empires have been cemented in blood.

> — EDMUND BURKE (1729–1797), *A Vindication of Natural Society,* 1756

Almost the whole of history is nothing but a series of horrors . . . [Tyrants] seem willing to allow the crimes of their predecessors to be transmitted to posterity, to divert attention from the horror that they themselves inspire. In fact, there is no longer any way of consoling the people except by teaching them that their forebears were as wretched as they are, or more so.

> — SÉBASTIEN-ROCH NICOLAS DE CHAMFORT (1741–1794), *Maxims and Thoughts,* 1796

If I live, I will fight, wherever I must, as long as I must, until the enemy is defeated and the national stain washed clean.

> — CHARLES DE GAULLE (1890–1970), *Les Mémoires de Guerre,* 1954

In war it is not just the weak soldiers, or the sensitive ones, or the highly imaginative or cowardly ones, who will break down. Inevitably, all break down if in combat long enough.

> — PAUL FUSSELL (1924–   ), *Wartime: Understanding and Behavior in the Second World War,* 1989

Such is the empire of Fortune . . . that it is almost equally difficult to foresee the events of war or to explain their various consequences.

> — EDWARD GIBBON (1737–1794), *The Decline and Fall of the Roman Empire,* 1776–1788

War is the admission of defeat in the face of conflicting interests.

> — GERMAINE GREER (1939–   ), *The Female Eunuch,* 1970

Internal strife is a thing much worse than war carried on by a united people, as war itself is worse than peace.

— HERODOTUS (ca. 484–after 424 B.C.), *The Persian Wars*

War has driven me. I think it's very deep in our genes. It drove me when I was younger. I think the question most men have is, "Am I a coward?" And the only way you can ever find out is to be in combat.

— DAVID MCCULLOUGH (1933–), interview with Roger Mudd, in *Great Minds of History,* 1999

The morning was still; the place was cool and pleasant.

Then a tremendous flash of light cut across the sky. Mr. Tanimoto has a distinct recollection that it traveled from east to west, from the city toward the hills. It seemed a sheet of sun.

— JOHN HERSEY (1914–1993), *Hiroshima,* 1946

Americans have characteristically judged their wars on the basis of their success. The best-known wars—the Revolution, the Civil War, and World War II—were all great successes. Although many people remembered the War of 1812 as a success, it was actually a failure, and perhaps this is why it attracts so little attention today.

— DONALD R. HICKEY (1944–), *The War of 1812: A Forgotten Conflict,* 1989

War has been the most convenient pseudo-solution for the problems of twentieth-century capitalism. It provides the incentives to modernisation and technological revolution which the market and the pursuit of profit do only fitfully and by accident, it makes the unthinkable (such as votes for women and the abolition of unemployment) not merely thinkable but practicable.... What is equally important, it can re-create communities of men and give a temporary sense to their lives by uniting them against foreigners and outsiders. This is an achievement beyond the power of the private enterprise economy . . . when left to itself.

— ERIC HOBSBAWM (1917–), *London Observer,* May 26, 1968

In peace, children inter their parents; war violates the order of nature and causes parents to inter their children.
— HERODOTUS (ca. 484–after 424 B.C.), *The Histories of Herodotus*

Politics must continue; war cannot. That is not to say that the role of the warrior is over. The world community needs, more than it has ever done, skillful and disciplined warriors who are ready to put themselves at the service of its authority. Such warriors must properly be seen as the protectors of civilisation, not its enemies. The style in which they fight for civilisation—against ethnic bigots, regional warlords, ideological intransigents, common pillagers and organised international criminals—cannot derive from the Western model of warmaking alone. Future peacekeepers and peacemakers have much to learn from alternative military cultures, not only that of the Orient but of the primitive world also. There is a wisdom in the principles of intellectual restraint and even of symbolic ritual that needs to be rediscovered. There is an even greater wisdom in the denial that politics and war belong within the same continuum. Unless we insist on denying it, our future . . . may belong to the men with bloodied hands.
— JOHN KEEGAN (1934–   ), *A History of Warfare*, 1993

There is no avoiding war; it can only be postponed to the advantage of others.
— NICCOLÒ MACHIAVELLI (1469–1527), *The Prince*, 1514

For among other evils caused by being disarmed, it renders you contemptible; which is one of those disgraceful things which a prince must guard against.
— NICCOLÒ MACHIAVELLI (1469–1527), *The Prince*, 1514

The main foundations of every state, new states as well as ancient or composite ones, are good laws and good arms . . . you cannot have good laws without good arms, and where there are good arms, good laws inevitably follow.
— NICCOLÒ MACHIAVELLI (1469–1527), *The Prince*, 1514

The world has never seen a more impressive demonstration of the influence of sea power upon its history. Those far distant, storm-beaten ships [of the British Royal Navy], upon which [Napoleon's] Grand Army never looked, stood between it and the dominion of the world.

— ALFRED THAYER MAHAN (1840–1914), *The Influence of Sea Power upon the French Revolution and Empire, 1793–1812*, 1892

War is what determines everything that follows. I mean, it mattered if Joshua Chamberlain held at Little Round Top or not. If he'd have crumbled, and if the Confederates had gotten down into Washington, we'd be in an entirely different world. So, war is decisive in a way that nothing else is. It determines who's going to determine the future.

— DAVID MCCULLOUGH (1933–   ), interview with Roger Mudd, in *Great Minds of History*, 1999

Television brought the brutality of war into the comfort of the living room. Vietnam was lost in the living rooms of America—not on the battlefields of Vietnam.

— MARSHALL MCLUHAN (1911–1980), in *Montreal Gazette*, May 16, 1975

All those who seek to destroy the freedom of the democratic nations must know that war is the surest and shortest means to accomplish this. That is the very first axiom of their science.

— ALEXIS DE TOCQUEVILLE (1805–1859), *Democracy in America*, 1840

You say it is the good cause that hallows every war? I tell you: it is the good war that hallows every cause.

— FRIEDRICH NIETZSCHE (1844–1900), *Thus Spoke Zarathustra*, 1884

War has always been the grand sagacity of every spirit which has grown too inward and too profound; its curative power lies even in the wounds one receives.

— FRIEDRICH NIETZSCHE (1844–1900), *Twilight of the Idols*, 1889

War is the supreme drama of a completely mechanized society.
  ⸺ LEWIS MUMFORD (1895–1990), *Technics and Civilization,* 1934

Those who know how to win are much more numerous than those who know how to make proper use of their victories.
  ⸺ POLYBIUS (ca. 200–ca. 118 B.C.), *History*

The pacifist is as surely a traitor to his country and to humanity as is the most brutal wrongdoer.
  ⸺ THEODORE ROOSEVELT (1858–1919), speech, July 27, 1917

Appeasement does not always lead to war; sometimes it leads to surrender.
  ⸺ WILLIAM SAFIRE (1929–   ), *The New York Times,* November 2, 1989

To plunder, to slaughter, to steal, these things [the Romans] misname empire; and where they make a wilderness, they call it peace.
  ⸺ TACITUS (ca. 55–ca. 120), *Agricola*

There are two things which will always be very difficult for a democratic nation: to start a war and to end it.
  ⸺ ALEXIS DE TOCQUEVILLE (1805–1859), *Democracy in America,* 1840

The only sure basis of an alliance is for each party to be equally afraid of the other.
  ⸺ THUCYDIDES (ca. 460–ca. 400 B.C.), *The Peloponnesian War*

At no point on the spectrum of violence does the use of combat offer much promise for the United States today. If the nuclear deterrent itself should fail, it is difficult to imagine the strategic nuclear forces as hurting, in Schelling's sense, without destroying. . . . Because the record of nonnuclear limited war in obtaining acceptable decisions at tolerable cost is also scarcely heartening, the history of usable combat may at last be reaching its end.
  ⸺ RUSSELL F. WEIGLEY (1930–   ), *The American Way of War,* 1977

The professional military mind is by necessity an inferior and unimaginative mind; no man of high intellectual quality would willingly imprison his gifts in such a calling.

— H. G. WELLS (1866–1946), *The Outline of History,* 1920

 *Women*

Man's discovery that his genitalia could serve as a weapon to generate fear must rank as one of the most important discoveries of prehistoric times, along with the use of fire and the first crude stone axe.

— SUSAN BROWNMILLER (1935–), *Against Our Will: Men, Women, and Rape,* 1975

The problem that has no name—which is simply the fact that American women are kept from growing to their full human capacities—is taking a far greater toll on the physical and mental health of our country than any known disease.

— BETTY FRIEDAN (1921–), *The Feminine Mystique,* 1963

It is easy to see that, even in the freedom of early youth, an American girl never quite loses control of herself; she enjoys all permitted pleasures without losing her head about any of them, and her reason never lets the reins go, though it may often seem to let them flap.

— ALEXIS DE TOCQUEVILLE (1805–1859), *Democracy in America,* 1840

Perhaps nothing is so depressing an index of the inhumanity of the male-supremacist mentality as the fact that the more genial human traits are assigned to the underclass: affection, response to sympathy, kindness, cheerfulness.

— KATE MILLETT (1934–), *Sexual Politics,* 1970

Is it too much to ask that women be spared the daily struggle for superhuman beauty in order to offer it to the caresses of a subhumanly ugly mate?

    — GERMAINE GREER (1939–   ), *The Female Eunuch,* 1970

The concept of romantic love affords a means of emotional manipulation which the male is free to exploit, since love is the only circumstance in which the female is (ideologically) pardoned for sexual activity.

    — KATE MILLETT (1934–   ), *Sexual Politics,* 1970

It is capitalist America that produced the modern independent woman. Never in history have women had more freedom of choice in regard to dress, behavior, career, and sexual orientation.

    — CAMILLE PAGLIA (1947–   ), "The Big Udder," 1991,
        reprinted in *Sex, Art, and American Culture,* 1992

In America a woman loses her independence forever in the bonds of matrimony. While there is less constraint on girls there than anywhere else, a wife submits to stricter obligations. For the former, her father's house is a home of freedom and pleasure; for the latter, her husband's is almost a cloister.

    — ALEXIS DE TOCQUEVILLE (1805–1859), *Democracy in America,*
        1840

I have no hesitation in saying that although the American woman never leaves her domestic sphere and is in some respects very dependent within it, nowhere does she enjoy a higher station. And . . . if anyone asks me what I think the chief cause of the extraordinary prosperity and growing power of this nation, I should answer that it is due to the superiority of their women.

    — ALEXIS DE TOCQUEVILLE (1805–1859), *Democracy in America,*
        1840

Work

A man perfects himself by working. Foul jungles are cleared away, fair seed-fields rise instead, and stately cities; and withal the man himself first ceases to be a jungle, and foul unwholesome desert thereby. . . . The man is now a man.

— THOMAS CARLYLE (1795–1881), *Past and Present*, 1843

We should not say that one man's hour is worth another man's hour, but rather that one man during an hour is worth just as much as another man during an hour. Time is everything, man is nothing: he is at the most time's carcass.

— KARL MARX (1818–1883), *The Poverty of Philosophy*, 1847

The production of too many useful things results in too many useless people.

— KARL MARX (1818–1883), *Economic and Philosophic Manuscripts*, 1844

In communist society, where nobody has one exclusive sphere of activity but each can become accomplished in any branch he wishes, society regulates the general production and thus makes it possible for me to do one thing today and another tomorrow, to hunt in the morning, fish in the afternoon, rear cattle in the evening, criticize after dinner, just as I have a mind, without ever becoming hunter, fisherman, shepherd or critic.

— KARL MARX (1818–1883) and FRIEDRICH ENGELS (1820–1895), *The German Ideology*, 1846

He who would do some great thing in this short life must apply himself to work with such a concentration of his forces as to idle spectators who live only to amuse themselves, looks like insanity.

— FRANCIS PARKMAN (1823–1893), quoted in Elbert Hubbard, *Elbert Hubbard's Scrap Book*, 1923

Give me a man who sings at his work.

— THOMAS CARLYLE (1795–1881), in Norman Vincent Peale,
My Favorite Quotations, 1990

A man willing to work, and unable to find work, is perhaps the
saddest sight that fortune's inequality exhibits under this sun.

— THOMAS CARLYLE (1795–1881), Chartism, 1839

Perhaps it is this specter that most haunts working men and
women: the planned obsolescence of people that is of a piece with
the planned obsolescence of the things they make.

— STUDS TERKEL (1912–   ), Working, 1972

We must cultivate our own garden. . . . When man was put in the
garden of Eden, he was put there so that he should work, which
proves that man was not born to rest.

— VOLTAIRE (1694–1778), Candide, 1759

Let us work without theorizing, 'tis the only way to make life
endurable.

— VOLTAIRE (1694–1778), Candide, 1759

⇌ *World War I* ⇋

The experience of the early warriors of 1914–1918—the probability of wounds or death, in circumstances of squalor and misery—swiftly acquired inevitability. . . . How did the anonymous millions, indistinguishably drab, undifferentially deprived of any scrap of the glories that by tradition made the life of the man-at-arms tolerable, find the resolution to sustain the struggle and to believe in its purpose? That they did is one of the undeniabilities of the Great War. Comradeship flourished in the earthwork cities of the Western and Eastern Fronts, bound strangers into the closest brotherhood, elevated loyalties created within the ethos of temporary regimentality to the status of life-and-death blood ties. Men whom the trenches cast into intimacy entered into bonds of mutual dependency and sacrifice of self stronger than any of the friendships made in peace and better times. That is the ultimate mystery of the first World War. If we could understand its loves, as well as its hates, we would be nearer understanding the mystery of human life.

　　—JOHN KEEGAN (1934–　　), *The First World War*, 1999

We are fighting in the quarrel of civilization against barbarism, of liberty against tyranny. Germany has become a menace to the whole world. She is the most dangerous enemy of liberty now existing.

　　— THEODORE ROOSEVELT (1858–1919), speech, April 1917

The nations were caught in a trap, a trap made during the first 30 days out of battles that failed to be decisive, a trap from which there was, and has been, no exit.

　　— BARBARA TUCHMAN (1912–1989), *The Guns of August*, 1962

When at last it was over, the war had many diverse results and one dominant one transcending all others: disillusion.

　　— BARBARA TUCHMAN (1912–1989), *The Guns of August*, 1962

The man who does not think it was America's duty to fight for her own sake in view of the infamous conduct of Germany toward us stands on a level with a man who wouldn't think it necessary to fight in a private quarrel because his wife's face was slapped.

—THEODORE ROOSEVELT (1858–1919), speech, April 1917

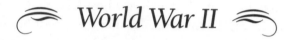

World War II

Hitler was certain that the kids that he had brought up in the Hitler Youth would always outfight the Boy Scouts. He thought of the American soldier as a spoiled son of democracy who could never be able to withstand the rigors of the modern battlefield. Hitler made a mistake.

—STEPHEN AMBROSE (1936–   ), interview with Roger Mudd, in *Great Minds of History*, 1999

One of my all-time favorite quotations from a GI came at the conclusion of an interview I was conducting, and I basically asked him [what he felt was at stake in World War II]. He answered, "Steve, I was nineteen years old. I had my life ahead of me. I knew the difference between right and wrong, and I didn't want to grow up in the world in which wrong prevailed."

—STEPHEN AMBROSE (1936–   ), interview with Roger Mudd, in *Great Minds of History*, 1999

Eisenhower got through the war on four hours of sleep a night, 20 cups of coffee a day, and four packs of Camel cigarettes, and an occasional sandwich. That's how we got through the war.

—STEPHEN AMBROSE (1936–   ), interview with Roger Mudd, in *Great Minds of History*, 1999

The Holocaust is a central event in many people's lives, but it has also become a metaphor for our century. There cannot be an end to speaking and writing about it.

— AHARON APPELFELD (1932–), *The New York Times,* November 15, 1986

We shall fight in France, we shall fight on the seas and oceans, we shall fight with growing confidence and growing strength in the air, we shall defend our island, whatever the cost may be, we shall fight on the beaches, we shall fight on the landing grounds, we shall fight in the fields and in the streets, we shall fight in the hills; we shall never surrender.

— WINSTON CHURCHILL (1874–1965), speech to the House of Commons, June 4, 1940

A single lurid fear brought the American decision to undertake the vast effort and expense to build the atomic bomb—the fear that Hitler's Germany would do it first.

— THOMAS POWERS (1940–), *Heisenberg's War: The Secret History of the German Bomb,* 1993

[Of his experience in the Holocaust:] I was the accuser, God the Accused. My eyes were open and I was alone—terribly alone in a world without God and without man.

— ELIE WIESEL (1928–), *Night,* 1958

Youth and Children

It were a real increase of human happiness, could all young men from the age of nineteen be covered under barrels, or rendered otherwise invisible; and there left to follow their lawful studies and callings, till they emerged, sadder and wiser, at the age of twenty-five.

— THOMAS CARLYLE (1795–1881), *Sartor Resartus,* 1833–1834

What society thinks and feels about its children is an index of its attitudes about a great number of things: knowledge, power, sex, the future.

— MARY GORDON, "Age of Innocents: The Cult of the Child," in Lorraine Glennon, ed., *Our Times: The Illustrated History of the 20th Century,* 1995

Index

·